But He Just Couldn't Breathe

Becoming A Doctor In Canada In The '60s

Seymour Tozman, MD
and
Neal Tozman

Wire Publishing

Copyright © 2017 by Wire Publishing. All rights reserved as this book may not be reproduced in whole or in part, by any means, without written consent of the publisher. For permission requests, write to the publisher, addressed "Attention: Permissions Coordinator" at the address below.

WIRE PUBLISHING & THE ULTIMATE PUBLISHING HOUSE
(TUPH) US HEADQUARTERS -
P.O. Box 1204, Cypress, Texas, U.S.A. 77410
205 Glen Shields Avenue, Toronto, Ontario, Canada L4K 2B0
Telephone: 647-883-1758
www.ultimatepublishinghouse.com
and
www.ButHeJustCouldntBreathe.com
E-mail: info@ultimatepublishinghouse.com

US OFFICE: Ordering Information
Quantity Sales: COMPANIES, ORGANIZATIONS, INSTITUTIONS,
AND INDUSTRY PUBLICATIONS.

Quantity discounts are available on bulk purchases of this book for reselling, educational purposes, subscription incentives, gifts, sponsorship, or fundraising. Unique books or book excerpts can also be fashioned to suit special needs such as private labeling with your logo on the cover and a message from or a message printed on the second page of the book. For more information, please contact our Special Sales Department at Wire Publishing/Ultimate Publishing House. Orders for college textbook or course adoption use.

Please contact Wire Publishing/Ultimate Publishing House Tel:
647-883-1758

Wire Publishing is a registered trademark of the Ultimate Publishing House - Printed in the United States

But He Just Couldn't Breathe by Dr. Seymour Tozman & Neal Tozman
ISBN - 978-0-692-88901-5

Contents

PART I
AN AUSPICIOUS BEGINNING

Chapter 1	Day One The Janitor	9
Chapter 2	First Love and Marny's Bottom, or, How Can I Do It If I Can't Even Breathe?	12
Chapter 3	Suicide: The Proper Technique & A Casualty	16
Chapter 4	The Teacher	20
Chapter 5	Orals and Anals	24
Chapter 6	And Genitals	28
Chapter 7	The Graveyard and the Grave	31
Chapter 8	Can You See The Forest?	34
Chapter 9	All Things Do End	36
Chapter 10	Gord Takes Pity	39
Chapter 11	Hurrah for Hollywood	43
Chapter 12	New York, New York	47
Chapter 13	The Autopsy; Tale of a Lily Liver	50
Chapter 14	The Eyes Have It	54
Chapter 15	The First Patient	57
Chapter 16	Trotsky Lives	59
Chapter 17	A Bad Omen	62

Chapter 18	O Say Can I See.	64
Chapter 19	But Can He Sing Soprano?	68
Chapter 20	Long John Silver	71
Chapter 21	Real Patients	74
Chapter 22	The Tea Party.	77
Chapter 23	Beating The Systems	79
Chapter 24	Practice Makes Perfect or, A Kick In Time . .	81
Chapter 25	The Precision of Science.	85
Chapter 26	The End is Near	88
Chapter 27	Light at the End of the Tunnel	90

PART II

THE INTERLUDE
or THEY PLAYED MUSIC BEFORE PEARL HARBOR

Chapter 1	Interlude: On the Road	95
Chapter 2	Bright Lights, Tight Tights	98
Chapter 3	Welcome to LA. We Stop for a Sandwich . . .	100
Chapter 4	Tijuana	102
Chapter 5	In The Pink	106
Chapter 6	Berkeley and The Nude Model	108

PART III

HEALER SEER DOER -PSYCHIATRIST, SURGEON, BLINDMAN, SEER

Chapter 1	Dracula—Is It All In Vein? 113
Chapter 2	Mount Sinai is Co-ed 116
Chapter 3	Vogel and His Birds 118
Chapter 4	A Firecracker 120
Chapter 5	A Routine Physical 122
Chapter 6	If you Ann, Does That Mean Me Tarzan 125
Chapter 7	Let's Try Type O .127
Chapter 8	To the Victor, the Spoils 129
Chapter 9	Saturday 132
Chapter 10	The Pacemaker or, There is No Charge for This 135
Chapter 11	Fair Trading 137
Chapter 12	Empathy and Euthanasia 139
Chapter 13	In the OR 142
Chapter 14	A Raven Beauty .144
Chapter 15	A Skilled Surgeon 146
Chapter 16	A Queasy Boner 148
Chapter 17	Where Were You . . . ? 152
Chapter 18	A Sight for Sore Eyes 153
Chapter 19	On the Couch 156
Chapter 20	Fate Has Spoken 159

Chapter 21	Other Crosses	161
Chapter 22	With Tongue in Cheek	164
Chapter 23	Clive and a Tough Customer	167
Chapter 24	Doublethink	170
Chapter 25	Gulliver's Travels	173
Chapter 26	A Surprise	176
Chapter 27	A Dying Child	178
Chapter 28	Hysteria and Placebo	179
Chapter 29	Youth and Power	181
Chapter 30	A Triangle	183
Chapter 31	Hysteria and Death	185
Chapter 32	The Epidemic	187
Chapter 33	A Cut Above the Rest	189
Chapter 34	Ward Work	193
Chapter 35	Anne	195
Chapter 36	More Slight Mistakes	198
Chapter 37	Birth and Rebirth	199

PART IV

EPILOGUE: Amerika, Amerika 202

PART I

AN AUSPICIOUS BEGINNING

1

Day One
The Janitor

Rain pelts the wide dusty windows splattering the heavy dirt and the neat graffiti which someone has managed to emblazon into the outside pane to frustrate the inside washers. I am hoping for an awful storm and cheer slightly as a flash of lightning momentarily reddens the sky followed by a rumble of distant thunder. I see, however, the peak fury of the elements has occurred and I am frustrated that it cannot match my mood nor will distract me from the offering on the table beside me.

My romance with the elements ends for good when a voice that startles me far more than lightning breaks the reverie as Wally calls out to the blue smocked janitor industriously rearranging odd shaped objects in a corner of the room.

"Hey," he shouts. "Fellah, we need you here."

What purpose my manicky colleague has in beckoning to this preoccupied menial and thus disturbing my meditation escapes me, nor does the janitor seem to much care to be thus disjointed from the work which he no doubt considers essential to the completion of his mission if not ours. I was just coming to realize that janitors really ran things, later to discover of course that the power was at least equally shared with secretaries and other clerks. It struck me then that Wally's impertinence could cost us dearly at some point with this menial man. Nevertheless, the youth persisted, allaying his own tension by ridiculing this laborer no doubt of lower caste or at least considerably less fortunate than he himself and myself too for that matter.

You can just imagine my extreme annoyance when I see the elderly individual is not taking the friendly jibing in any exceptionally good spirits as why in the world should he.

"You there," he says in a rather too stern voice considering who we are and who he is. "You boys would do much better to stop horsing around and read your texts for the next ten minutes."

"I'll be with you then!"

Wally's face is suffused for a moment with a kind of shock. "Hey," he whispers, "who is that guy?"

"You shmucks," whispers another student pluralizing you will note to all four of us partners now in a peccadillo of no small proportion. "That's Professor Adams, the Director of the lab."

Such was our start as we embarked on our medical career. Bad, no horrid, was the task ahead. Possibly none would survive.

And least likely me I think, poor with bad eyes and a queasy stomach and we were already the shmucks of the year.

How could this have happened to me? I ask you that. Do you think I wanted this for a career? I am here because of my ethnic origin ineluctably Judaic despite orthodox atheism, and only just beginning to date even non-kosher young ladies (i.e., "shiksas"), after a diet, which hitherto forbade such delicacies.

Be that as it may. We all turn our attention to the great and heavy tomes that lay about and with fever burning try to make some sense of their contents. It's no use. The books are too heavy and the vocabulary foreign and I am hopelessly lost beyond redemption and wish to die. I regard the horrible package on the slab and a sense of numbness overtakes me and I ask myself why am I not fainting. But the question cannot linger long, as my other friends, Ken and Shel, undrape the vinyl tarp (suitably black) to reveal Sir Morton, an antique oil soaked cadaveric looking specimen, in fact a cadaver, the first of its kind I have ever seen.

I wish you to know that this is indeed a special occasion, for I am for the first time facing Death, my nemesis. I have seen Him before when he took my gentle grandfather, but I have never touched Him nor confronted so concretely his essence. And here was He then in the person of this wizened and shrunken and foul smelling object who was for one year to be my closest companion and the fifth though silent member of our four man team.

Please, Dear God, where is the storm? Where is something to break the tension? God does oblige with a half hearted rumble of thunder but the seas do not part for me and I am not saved. And Professor Adams still disguised as a janitor has returned.

Stern orders are issued and instructions given and almost to my relief there is no more time for philosophy, not now, not ever. We are immersed in anatomy for the duration, and there will be no more idle thought. We must cut the corpus and learn its peculiar geography and pass a barrage of examinations or else never be doctors and what else was I to be? Thus, I, a youth frightened and fearful of Death, who walked in childhood blocks out of my way to avoid a funeral home, am now confronted with the presence of a cadaver and intimately so, living and breathing and surrounded by Death.

We have begun the dissection of the posterior triangle of the neck. Professor Adams thinks we are silly young boys, but we have survived the first day, and perhaps some of us will be doctors, even me.

I leave the lab numb and reeking with the smell of Death, which will not wash off for the whole year. The rain has stopped as I make my way home and streaks of red like searing wounds are in the sky.

2

First Love and Marny's Bottom,

or, How Can I Do It If I Can't Even Breathe?

It is long ago. I am sitting in class watching Marny Carter's beautiful bottom peeping out of her blue gym bloomers as she stands a few seats ahead, trying to intelligently answer a question in Social Studies. All us boys however are concentrating on her ass, its firm symmetry beckoning us like luscious fruit.

Alas, it is forbidden fruit for more reasons than one. She is non-Jewish and I cannot yet cope with crossing racial lines even to pluck so juicy a morsel. Moreover, I am a "brain," bookish and serious, and she plays with the jocks. Also, I am too tongue-tied, skinny, immature and hopeless. She couldn't possibly be interested in someone like me. Damn it, I wonder if she does anything with the other boys. There are rumors.

Marny tries to answer skinny spinster Miss Pruit's sharp questioning and vainly attempts to appear intelligent. She is somehow not very convincing at this; however, we boys don't mind.

She and the other cheerleaders are in blue gym bloomers since next class is practice for them, and I and the other boys are studiously watching the fine lithe legs as she self consciously shifts her weight from one leg to the other. Oh rapture, I am three seats behind her. Look at her pert little ass peeking out from her bloomers. How round it is! Is it talking to me? Why have I not the confidence and flair of someone like Wally? Wally steps in front of Millie, another cheerleader, with a sweet, lithe body, dark curly hair and dark eyes. This is on the football field and the girls are in their red outfits with tiny skirts, red panties and pompom boots.

Marny is there too, flirting with Solly Kelner, the quarterback.

God, how I want those ladies. I hate football but attend all the games to see the cheerleaders. It is the only place to see skin these days, for all the girls normally wear long crinolines and keep their shakables stabilized with tight corsetry.

Wally sniffs Millie's curly hair. "Hey, whatcha do that for?"

"Aren't you glad I'm not a doggie?"

Millie laughs red faced and gives him a playful smack in the face. Christ, I could never say that to a girl.

Marny finally sits down. She is embarrassed and someone else answers the question. Somebody should be doing something with that girl. Somebody must be. It turns out nobody is. They are all intimidated, like me, and we find to our dismay, that she quickly goes down with an American guy from Albany who is a year younger than we are. He is part of the one week exchange student program with the U.S. Not suffering from Toronto paralysis, he asks Marny to fuck him and apparently (allegedly) she says OK.

Now here is a really sad story. Linda was my dream girl. She was my Elizabeth Taylor. (I fell in love with Elizabeth Taylor at age seven when I saw Courage of Lassie). Linda had dark straight hair and soft white skin, and she had violet eyes like my movie star goddess. I first saw Linda in public school. She was a year behind me and her class shared part of our room for a time. I watched her emerging femininity and tasted her with my eyes when she stood to quietly and capably answer a question. So enamored with her was I that I actually got up the nerve to ask her for a date. I was at VRCI (Vaughan Road Collegiate) by now, age fifteen.

Linda was so beautiful and sweet, bittersweet. She was my first date.

I guess I was not her first, at least I assumed so pretty a girl would be terribly popular. But she was quiet and shy, so perhaps maybe she was not (so popular). Did she like me too?

Is it possible she did? Oh, why do I have this breathing difficulty? Why can I not breathe when I want something so badly?

At her home she greets me at the door. She is wearing a pretty yellow cocktail dress with flowers. And it is scooped out to reveal a cleft of actual bosom beneath, gently dewily straining at the material. Her dark hair, shiny clean and soft, glistened, framing her luminescent face and white skin. An Elizabeth Taylor doll only fourteen years old. I gasped for breath as I tasted with my eyes this strange entity. A delicate vision with rounded bosoms so tenderly held up by the filamentous laces of her dress, beneath which and only just visible was a white bra strap.

Not wanting to appear to be lasciviously looking down into the sweet sight, I cast my eyes further to her shoes. They were pretty with shiny sequins.

At a loss for words I remark "Oh, you have pretty shoes…"

"I wore them for you."

Oh Lord, I am doomed. Glass slippers! Do I still have a glass slipper?

At the bus stop "Why, you are trembling."

"Yes, yes it's cold." I as manly as possible reply.

But I am not trembling for cold, I am trembling for Linda, barely fifteen years old.

We go to Nortown Cinema and we see The Country Girl. I choose this film because Grace Kelly was so delectable in Rear Window.

She had rosy red lips that came at you across the whole screen and I, in my mind, returned the kiss with passion. But in this movie, she looks ugly, grotesque. Or is it me? Linda seems to be crying. Is she moved by this film? She is soft and sensitive. I cannot concentrate on the screen, for I am fervently trying to determine how to lower my right arm lying across the back of her chair onto her white neck and shoulders. She has bare shoulders and I can see two delicate straps, one from the white bra below. I cannot drop my arm to her back since it has turned to wood and is becoming numb.

I awkwardly move it, raising it in a salute to the Fuehrer, and shift my position. Now my hand is in my lap. Grace is shouting at Bing to stop his drinking and I am gradually, inexorably moving my right hand up to the arm rest level, eyeing Linda's soft white hand glowing in the dark in her lap. Finally, I pounce. Suddenly, my hand is in hers and she lets out a stifled yelp. I turn my lips up into a smile and am glad it is dark so she cannot see the twitch. Eventually, I let go.

The snow crunches under us and I deliver her home. I brush her lips with mine. My first kiss of a strange girl. Her perfume, cologne intoxicates me. I tell her she is pretty because men are supposed to do that, though I say it so fast she probably mishears or thinks I am incoherent. I wave goodbye and am greatly relieved now to be on the street alone. I am sweating and cold. Now I am trembling for cold.

I try again with Linda, this time a dance. But I cannot dance—certainly not with Linda. I cannot even breathe. Finally, I cannot take it anymore and do not call her again. She thinks I do not like her and I could not even breathe. Linda, I loved you, I was crazy about you. But I just couldn't breathe.

Thanks to Leila's matchmaking, I am sitting on the couch with this girl.

"Hey," she remarks, "you're not much of a lover." That was for laughing at Martha Raye on TV in the middle of a kiss.

"I'm sorry," I say, "I'll do better."

But I am not in the right mood. I need the proper circumstances. I cannot do this with her father snoring in the next room. Besides, there is something about her looks that isn't right. She is not delicate enough. I like delicate girls with fine bones and she doesn't seem to have a neck or a waist. If she had that, it would make a difference. Her boobs are very large and I can feel them all I want and everything else too.

She is breathing too hard. The situation just isn't right. I may be desperate but I'm still particular.

Did the dancing lessons do any good? Six lessons at an introductory rate. Well, I don't kick quite as hard and Leila, the instructress, said I have 'natural rhythm.' Perhaps she mistakes my color? I am not even tanned as Harvey Kopman (a Toronto Jew) was when he had to ride the back of the bus on his trip to Mississippi.

3

Suicide: The Proper Technique & A Casualty

We are being entertained today with a droll lecture. It started with sporadic levity, a Playboy centerfold pasted on the blackboard displaying an exceedingly voluptuous young woman. Professor Duckworth, taking the prank in stride, is giving us a lecture in surface anatomy, and pointing out (with a pointer) the hypertrophied mammary organs of the unfortunate female and how poorly her endowments were adapted to their primary function of giving milk. He does not however dwell on their usefulness for suckling medical students.

I am going blind you know. No, it is true. I have an eye condition and have terrible astigmatism. The eye doctor says I'm an interesting case. I have to sit near the front to copy the diagrams, which appear rapidly on the blackboard simplifying if one is speedy enough to copy well, what is detailed in a morass of textbook words.

Professor Duckworth has shifted now from oversized anatomical globes to a discussion of the carotid artery. He informs us that bending one's head forward rather than back makes prominent these major vessels. He points out that this is a common error in suicide attempts, merely producing tracheal nicking rather than arterial slicing. He advises us should we wish to do away with ourselves in this manner, be sure to bend the head forward. Two years ago, a young woman student had killed herself in this manner, "and properly so, since she had straight As in Anatomy." In fact, the good professor goes on, there has statistically been one suicide for each graduating year and he predicts one of my colleagues will die this way before we finish school. We cannot wait to see if he will be right.

Next week is our first Anatomy oral, the first oral examination any of us has had.

I am worried about Byron. He is a friend and I see he has become very withdrawn in the last couple of weeks. I have a feeling he cannot take this cadaver business. It is dirty work and irreverent too. He has had a pretty much sheltered, Orthodox Jewish upbringing and moreover likes things neat and clean and this hardly fulfills that criterion. He and I did much commiserating last year particularly when it came to our Zoo course, which was run by Adolph Hitler himself. The biology of animals is a fascinating subject, but in the hands of Professor Adolph, was a terror course, failing large numbers of second year students. That was little Benjy's downfall and that particular classmate was spending a second year in Pre-Med right now thanks to Adolph. Benjy was a pain in the ass and had bad breath besides but ought to have got through. Byron endured Zoo with its dirty dissections of frogs, snakes and rabbits. He endured the indignities of failing the terror ridden examinations including one where this brilliant student who had entered medical school with one of the highest averages in the province, attained a sixteen out of one hundred on a surprise test. That was not as bad as Roy who had pulled seven out of one hundred, but then Roy had labeled a drawing of a rabbit upside down realizing his mistake at the very end of the exam with loud exclamations.

These exams did not ultimately count for much but represented psychological torture and indeed, one frail student, a dark eyed Venezuelan girl, actually did go crazy and spent time in the nuthouse after a few months of Adolph's treatment.

Practical exams in Zoo were awful 'bell ringers' where one had two minutes to answer ten questions on an obscure specimen and then at the sound of a bell as loud as a fire alarm, had to move on to the next. Dr. Adolph had the grades on a sliding scale so as it turned out, a forty out of one hundred became eighty out of one hundred or else everyone failed. One got part marks for a close answer, but as Adolph put it, "The person who called the nostril of the snake its anus got no marks."

Byron spent most of his time in Zoo trading jokes with one Bentley B. Bentley, now no longer with us having failed everything. Byron and he had a huge list of anti-Jewish, anti-Christian jokes, which Byron regularly transmitted to me. "And so the priest sprinkled his car with holy water, thereupon the rabbi rushed out to his car with metal scissors and cut the tailpipe off…!"

Now I can see Byron is depressed. Zoo was dirty, but here we are, doing it to a person, not a snake and Byron cannot endure it I think. I hear from his teammate that he is thinking of dropping out of medical school.

"Byron, is that true?" I ask. "I heard this rumor." "Nah, nah, it's not true," Byron answers.

I am reassured for Byron is a friend. Does one not turn to friends when in distress? I tell my own teammates. "No, Byron won't drop out."

Next day, I learn Byron has dropped out. I am saddened by the loss and my sense of friendship is shaken. I realize Byron is a little strange and though I admire his fine mind and maintain a friendship as he enters Law and ultimately becomes a professor growing in stature and girth simultaneously, finally the friendship withers and he is gone from my life forever.

But back to business. Wally is shouting at me.

"No, Fingers (nickname from Toes-man), no! You are cutting the cutaneous nerves. We will never pass the oral if we can't see anything."

"Listen, you prick," I say, "We're not anatomists. We don't need to know every piddling nerve, do we? Besides, I can't see the friggin' things anyway."

It was of course all I could do to keep my contact lenses from bouncing up onto my sclera since my corneas were irregular or worse, they could fall out onto the corpse.

"Alright, alright," shouts Wally, "you don't do it, we'll do it."

The others agree, so I am relegated to watching the intricate manoeuvres, though I continue to cut and poke at the grosser structures. The oral is approaching and I do not wish to disgrace my team or my family or myself.

Byron, wait for me, I'm coming too.

4

The Teacher

"Here, take a look at these," He pressed them at the young pupil,(me) who intrepidly regarded the photos creased and faded as they were. It took a second or two to make out what was going on and then a degree of shock as I realize that the pretty face with its bared breasts has a thick genital organ of the opposite sex in its mouth.

"Geez," I say, "I didn't know people do that!"

Frank is very pleased at this response and indicates he has known this all along even though is barely a year older than me, at sixteen.

"Is this sanitary?" I ask, too amazed to be aroused at this sight.

"C'mon, it's fun, you should try it."

As the decrepit auto chugs up the road, Frank tells me of the beautiful girl he picked up.

"You have to try and relax when you do it," he says, "I had trouble at first, but I lay on my back and let her do it and it was fine."

"Here," he says, "no, you have to let the gear pause in neutral," as the car makes a grinding noise in protest.

I am in a sweat with the ordeal of trying to keep the car on the road this time, as Frank goes on with the description.

"Then," he is saying, "she just bent over and lifted her skirt up and she had nothing underneath and she says, 'Do you like?' and I say, 'Yeah' and, 'go crazy.'"

Despite my real concern with keeping the seventy five dollar 1938 jalopy (a 1938 Olds Coupe) steady, these salacious characterizations have their effect. The image of a beautiful pantiless lady bending over with skirt raised and asking provocatively, "Do you like it?" stays with me in fact over the years, well forever, to be honest.

I must concentrate on driving this car. My parents were crazy to give permission for me to buy it. It could be the end of me. Already, we have been in a ditch, and after a bump in the road on Dufferin Street, we sprawled across the opposite lane of traffic forcing cars to halt with screeching brakes. How lucky the highway wasn't too crowded or we would both be dead.

Now here we were again in traffic at night traveling up Dufferin Street slowly and painfully. Dimly, as Frank banters on, I realize there is a lot of traffic behind me and little in front and am relieved when Frank tells me to turn off the main road onto a side street. As I make my way up a small rise, I am overtaken by another auto and I discern waving.

"Hey, hey, pull over," murmurs Frank.

The car starts to wobble as we head for a ditch again. Frank grabs the wheel and I slam on the brakes throwing him against the windshield. It's the cops!

"Alright, you two," and to me, "Let's see your license Sonny." I sheepishly offer my driving permit.

"Are you his father?" asks one of the two officers of Frank sitting quietly in his seat.

Frank is deeply insulted given his own tender age (now seventeen), though a burly youth, a Hungarian "freedom fighter" with thinning blond hair. He has a chauffeur's license though, and the police are impressed.

"Yeah," they say of me, "I guess he has to learn somewhere. But try and stay off the main highway if you can. You've been holding up a line of traffic."

The cops depart. "Cheez, are you hopeless," says Frank, "you almost went into the ditch again. Didn't you see those were cops?" Frank is angry and insulted I presume at having been mistaken for my father, and the lesson is over for tonight. Though somewhat humiliated I am smiling for my father of seventeen was so funny.

"Hey Phil. Let me see it." Phil Kessel is flashing a photo around the class and I want to see it too. Wally had showed me a deck of cards, which had fifty two porno shots on it.

"Geez," he had remarked, "that girl looks just like my sister." It was a photo of a pretty dark haired girl, naked on a bed putting a bottle into her dark pubic region. "I can't believe this," Wally kept saying.

Now Phil has a photo and of course I want to see it. Phil is a poor student and will drop out of high school soon but he is a jock and shows he gets the girls. He shows me the picture.

God, it is a picture of Ettie, Ettie Kane. She is naked and bending over looking at the camera displaying everything. Her face is unsmiling and made up and I am absolutely goggle-eyed. Ettie is a senior one year ahead of us in high school. My God, she's even Jewish and a prefect too. I cannot pass her in the hall without visions of her beautiful and bold ass etched into my mind. How I wished I could jump her or rape her. What a beautiful wicked girl! (If only they were all like that!).

"Look, Frank, I have never been out in a canoe. I don't think this is a very good idea."

"Come on, there's nothing to it," argues my husky Hungarian friend.

He hops into the canoe and beckons me. I reluctantly accede to his pressure and go in and he shoves off. We proceed slowly and smoothly for a few minutes till we are some one hundred yards from shore. Suddenly, the canoe tilts and it is listing badly.

"Balance it. Balance," yells Frank. I move to balance but in the wrong direction and we are suddenly practically horizontal. Chivalrously and I guess, feeling responsible for me because of my earlier protests, Frank jumps out, wearing the new blue suede shoes he had been displaying proudly just minutes before.

Aghast, I see him splashing and floundering fully dressed in the murky waters of the bay. He will drown. How can I save him? Abruptly, he stops thrashing and stands upright and lo, the water is only up to his waist. I burst out laughing and he does too and he pushes me to shore.

But his brand new blue suede shoes are wrecked forever, all curled up. He drives the car barefoot home. He never forgives me for this I think and after sporadic attempts to keep up with one another, my friend and the friendship fade slowly away, a casualty, I guess, of a curled up pair of blue suede shoes.

5

Orals and Anals

I am standing beside Sir Morton feeling very tense again, which is a condition that accompanies all of my medical training in varying degrees. Though some students eat lunch in the anatomy lab, I never do and, in fact, have little desire to eat at all. This keeps me nice and slim to the dismay of relatives who would like nothing better than a fat doctor, I divine.

There is often great levity in the anatomy lab, stemming one would suppose from a need to divest oneself from the reality of what one was doing. The cadavers did not seem real, and regrettably, were not treated as if they had ever thought or felt or were even somebody's child. Most (when they were recognizable at all beyond their sallow wrinkled condition), did not appear to be Caucasian, but rather from assorted exotic and distant races, which seemed to make their dehumanization easier. Occasionally, I am ashamed for my colleagues to relate, their iconoclastic revelry was such as to entail throwing tissue, large pieces of dissected human skin, or other pieces of meat about the room at one another. Other pranksterism of even worse nature (which in the interests of taste, I'll forego) also occurred from time to time. Well, what could one expect? We were young. It was difficult, no impossible, systematically, day in and day out to chop into a corpse and be not inured nor affected in some way. Further there is an understated realization of the inevitability of Death, that one day that condition, such incredible horror, will be our own fate.

Sir Morton is now beginning to look the worse for wear. His neck and upper limbs have been dissected out and his arms display naked tendons and arteries and nerves. It is strange. You can pull on a tendon at the upper forearm, and the corresponding finger would move, like a type of marionette. Thus, when I run over to Nadine H. and say, "Look, I can make my fingers move," pressing thusly my upper forearm. She wide-eyed thinks I am really manipulating my tendons, since so it is on our cadavers.

And when I then do a piano motion with my right hand on my left wrist, correspondingly moving my left fingers frenetically she, realizing it is a joke, bursts into gales of laughter. This joke, incidentally, works only on anatomy students who have dissected the forearm.

Well, here am I again feeling nauseous and a victim. Shelly, one of my three partners, is waiting with me as we watch Dr. Granger slowly make his way counterclockwise round the tables, heading inexorably for us, though we are the last of the five tables in our room.

As Dr. Granger questions the groups of students ahead of us, Shel and I watch the proceedings (petrified ourselves), which though out of earshot are in clear visible range. I watch the white-faced students moving to demonstrate motions and actions of muscles on this first oral ever.

How scared we all are!

As I stand by the cadaver, I watch Karl making a motion to Dr. Granger, putting his arm forward, then back. Dr. Granger shakes his head and Karl tries again making a more circular motion, which this time is closer. The Professor corrects him demonstrating a complex motion. I feel ill. I am not even sure what muscle that would be. The Trapezius? No, that would lift up.

The Scalenus? The Serratus? I don't know. I am very worried.

Finally, after relentless, endless progression, it is our turn. Shel is questioned first and seems to be holding his own. There is some head shaking and corrections but I am relieved he is doing moderately well, since perhaps that will be good for me. That is, Dr. G. will think we are competent at this table. On the other hand, this could make things very difficult for me, since I could look bad by contrast. What will happen?

Suddenly, Dr. Granger asks Shelly, "Okay, can you describe the action of the Serratus Anterior?" Shel gamely tries, moving his arm forward and back, but he clearly does not know.

"Do you know?" asks the Professor looking at me. I am momentarily paralyzed, then slowly move my arm forward, then around in a complex motion as I had seen him do minutes before with Karl.

"That's very good," says the Professor, to my great astonishment and Shelly's too.

Things go well from there, I think, for my tendon games have paid off, and I know the muscles of the arm and soon the nerveracking experience is over. Shelly and I head for home ennervated, dysphoric and beyond coherent speech.

When the grades are posted one week later, I anxiously make my way to view the damage. Good Lord, I can't find my name in the pass column. Could my judgment be so out of whack? I look at the fail column but my eyes are swimming. I am almost in tears. A kind hand sympathetically pats my back and a voice says it is Karl -

"Geez, how did you ever do that?" I follow his gaze to the top of the first column and there is my name by itself. I have got the highest mark in the class on our first oral ever.

For a while, my buddies, remembering high school, are worried I may try to make a comeback, (I heard Roy say, "Watch out for Tozman, he's making a comeback!") but this is dispelled a month or so later in our second oral when Dr. Duckworth himself examines me. He, the head of the department, seems unaware of my past glories. Don't you know who I am? Deprecatingly, he asks a series of questions, which get simpler and simpler as I fumble. Finally, "Do you know where the gallbladder is?"

The experience is humiliating and though I am glad to receive a passing grade, I note with some embarrassment that my name on the posted list is once again by itself at the end of the pass list just above the red fail line.

A variable performance one might say on two orals, again a pattern that holds true for me throughout medical school. I seem to be surviving however.

6

And Genitals

I don't know how this has happened but Husky is in love with a goblet cell. He is sitting beside me in histology class and is making peculiar guttural noises, which can only be described as ecstatic as he peers with eagerness into his microscope. What a pain to have this looney beside me so eager and loving his work.

"Look! Look!" he exclaims, "See its round bottle shape and the cilia tool."

You would think he was describing a girl! For my part, the goblet cells do not turn me on nor does any of the drudgery of the course, which requires peering into the microscope seeing the structures and drawing them in a book. Later we would be tested on the structures. Why do some of my microscope drawings look like a high power view of a contact lens? Shades of Thurber.

But today, we will break the monotony. Roy has tickets for the Lux and we are going to cut out early to catch a special matinee. Even Husky is coming along although I suspect the histology of the intestinal tract is far more interesting to him. I guess he will make a really fine doctor someday. I don't know what will become of me, putting girls ahead of goblet cells.

We are sitting in the Lux burlesque house. We are a raucous bunch of medical students having an especially good time, for we have got free tickets for the matinee and the star performer, Dolly Bubbles, is Ray's former classmate, Gladys Shapiro from Bathurst Heights Collegiate (a.k.a. high school). It is an occasion when one finds a Jewish girl a burlesque star in Toronto, let alone one someone has gone to school with. It renews one's hope that perhaps some of the girls one has been dating and getting nowhere with might latently be available strippers and whores. I thank Gladys for this fantasy though this would be the first and last time I meet her (if one calls this a meeting).

We are watching the trailer film, which is a ludicrously bad one with Victor Mature as the beleaguered hero battling the terrible "Khan," evoking booing the hero and cheering the villain. The Khan is promptly labeled "Garbage Khan" more or less to the amusement of the other rain-coated patrons in the theater.

These, one must remember, were the days in Toronto when people still travelled the one hundred miles to Buffalo for kicks, so the situation was all the more unusual. "Dirty movies" were seen only surreptitiously in the frat house basement for a high fee to pay for the illegal film and the risks involved. And one watched the salacious fare ever fearing the surrogates and protectors of society would bust in and bust us. This however today was legal unless Dolly Bubbles would do something special for her special fans.

Finally, it is show time, which proceeds through a number of tame acts including inescapable and perfunctory vaudeville routines. At long last, Dolly appears and wearing a little girl outfit.

She looks like a lot of the nice Jewish girls I was dating and that is a charge. "Yay, Gladys," shout a number of the students who know her, as she goes into her act. She realizes she has a special audience so puts a lot into her act—gyrating and wiggling though not losing her pasties as we hope she might.

As she arches her back onto the stage with legs apart and does a deft somersault, Roy shouts up, "Hey Gladys, you were always good in gym."

She professionally ends her act with a bemused smile at probably her liveliest audience to date. I have taken in her lithe body with tiny waist and huge boobs and wonder what Professor Duckworth would have to say about this anatomical presentation.

The show is over. When the lights go on, we head out of the theater leaving the first two rows, which we have all occupied. As our eyes acclimatize to the brightness, we observe, sitting sedately in the back row, one of our own top anatomy professors, McDougal. It seems all the anatomists are very dedicated to their work and would not miss an opportunity to view a good specimen.

7

The Graveyard and the Grave

I force myself to look at the deep grave. Its walls are reddish from the clay-like soil, and there is a high mound of earth to the side waiting to be cast atop the coffin of a person only just dead. This is very frightening to me for I have never before been in a graveyard. Mother, knowing my inordinate fear is trying to de-condition her nine year old child who still must circle several blocks out of his way to visit Uncle Max's pharmacy, which has in its path en route the McDougal and Brown Funeral Parlor, Inc. Sometimes, I would nervously go past the parlor, furtively hoping I would beat the arrival of the somber long black van, and the retinue of tear streaked and wailing mourners. Where I got this fear I do not know, for I had no exposure to death and only heard people talk of it. If (Lord forbid) I should look on a corpse perhaps I should turn to stone. But no, really, it was the fetish of death I feared, not so much the corpse itself.

Now as I looked agonizingly at the open grave, I was in terror lest a hearse black and shiny and with slow inexorability would arrive and somberly disgorge a shiny polished casket and grief-stricken silent mourners would carry it to the grave and cover it with dirt. I could feel the pain of the mourners and did not know if I could bear it. (Our cadaver has, so far as I know, no relatives, you see.)

Finally, we leave the cemetery. There were no mourners or funerals and the day is sunny and bright. I run off and play, and later, at the beach where we are staying at my aunt's cottage in Port Huron, Michigan, they are singing "Cruising Down the River," and then "Four Leaf Clover." (Emmy Rossum sings it now). Whenever I hear those tunes I think about the open grave and its red walls.

I am fourteen. I am in the Benjamin's Funeral Home. I am staring numbly at the casket in which my dear grandfather Paisee (for Passover – Pasquale if Italian, I understand) is lying.

His arms are folded peacefully across his chest and he wears a yarmulke and white tallis. My mother is weeping quietly, and I am too stricken to weep. He was a good man and died of prostate cancer, in such pain. I watched him die in horrible fascination. He thought his pharmacist son Maxie would do magic and save him, but we were all helpless against the cancer that wracked his body. My mother blamed the orthopaedic doctor, Dr. Shapiro for putting him in that whole body cast for his "arthritis" when it was cancerous metastases. But Dr. Shapiro, I found later, was a dedicated man and tried his best to save him though it all went wrong!

I saw him slip away and did not kiss him goodbye the day he died. I just came into the hospital room and stared speechless like the others as he trailed into a final stupor. He had rallied a few days before when my aunt came in from Michigan and he cried when he saw her swollen belly. "You already have a name for me," he wept as he regarded what was indeed to be his namesake (Paul) growing in her loins.

I left the room for a few minutes and ate something outside the hospital. When I returned he had passed away. I do wish I had not left before I could say goodbye. (Oh, why didn't I say goodbye?)

As I stand by the coffin exhausted and numb, I stare at his face, rouged and rosy in sharp contrast to the sallow appearance recently in life. But see beneath, the gray. The eyes are closed at peace at last and the lips seem tranquil red and almost alive except for a funny twist indicating the final rigor. I stare at the peaceful chest with its hands folded across. He is not wearing his worn gold ring, I have it. It is given to me. As I stare, his chest seems to move. "Look, ma," I say and then I fall silent embarrassed, for I realize my mind is playing tricks. He is gone. I help carry the gray coffin to the hearse and to the open grave. It is so heavy I can hardly lift it.

But I was Bar Mitzvahed now and a man. The coffin sinks into the ground with the Hebrew Kaddish chanting. Then earth is thrown onto the coffin making a hollow sound. With that my Zaida was gone forever. Goodbye, my Zaida, goodbye.

8

Can You See The Forest?

It is a long climb to the top of the stairs up to the anatomy lab, situated on the topmost floor like an artist's studio. And what are we sculpting up there? I am breathing heavily as I reach the top of the landing returning from a brief respite.

The climb could give you pneumothorax I have been told. I am a veteran now; I have seen it all. There is little that can faze me. But somehow returning after a break is almost like starting over. The cadaveric smell was just beginning to diminish and now I am back to the drudgery and the anxiety and the pressure and the bad eyes and the smell. Ugh, smell it now.

Ken has clambered up and is beside me and he and I are about to enter the lab around the corner. We seem to be the first ones here. That doesn't happen very often. I am more often the last one in—especially if it's a morning class—like the time I made a grand entrance in the physics sound class at the end of the Marseillaise, covered in snow, and received an ovation from the class.

Oh, I don't want to be here. I pause at the door. Now Larry is coming along. What will happen to us next? Poor Larry, he almost got washed out last year in Premeds. I have known him since grade nine we were in the same form and I saw he was absent the morning of the Philosophy final.

"Where's Larry?" I had asked Ken. "What could have happened to him?"

After the exam, we called his home and his mother said he wasn't there; he had gone to school.

We rushed to the library, worried now that something had happened to the poor sap and there in a back room of the medical wing was Larry, pacing the floor and reading his philosophy books. He looked up and said, "Hi guys, what's up?"

"Larry, are you studying Philosophy?" "Yeh, why...?"

"Larry, I'm sorry to tell you we've just come from the exam. It was this morning, not in the afternoon."

"Oh God, oh no..."

Larry saw the Dean, a stern Scottish military man and was berated as he never had been before in his life. "And you expect to be a doctor?" But with the philosophy prof's approbation, he was allowed to buy his own personal exam, which he took alone and passed. So here he was still, though a little the worse for wear.

I have dallied as long as I can and I cautiously peer around the corner through the open door of the lab to see if our friends are still there.

There I see a sight I shall not soon forget. Sir Morton and all the rest are in the lithotomy position. The cadavers are obscenely laid out on their backs with legs spread and high in the air. A grotesque forest of cadaver legs. A horrific array of cadaver whores in a brothel of Hell.

The cadavers are so arranged for us to dissect the perineal (ano-genital) area. We laugh hysterically and try to joke but even the most irreverent of us cannot formulate coherently a proper gallows humor response to this. Veterans that we are, inured to our peculiar confrontation with Death, this display has floored us immeasurably. It is impressed in my mind as the most bizarre image of my life.

9

All Things Do End

I cannot believe it! The first year is over. I do not have to look at Sir Morton ever again. No never! And, wondrous to relate, I have passed. Our final practical examination in Anatomy has passed into oblivion, and what do you know, my team has had a distinction! You see, we had a friend on the inside, on the practical. Yes, Sir Morton himself was there. It seems my group had dissected the ocular orbit in an exemplary way (having totally botched the easier gross structures) and there was our own cadaver, his ocular orbit bared and a little red string around the trochlear nerve, meticulously dissected out. We got no prize for this but it was an honor nonetheless to have our specimen selected for the final practical examination. We were not even consulted, but there was Sir Morton, question five.

It reminded me of the rabbit dissection in physiology when we had so botched the dissection that we put our anesthesized rabbit out of its misery with a whopping dose of intraperitoneal urethane, and went to lunch abandoning the experiment. When we returned, we found that we had now, not succeeded in killing our poor rabbit, but that it was the only one still alive and was to be used to demonstrate how to complete the procedures everyone was supposed to have carried out. For having abandoned the experiment for "humane" reasons, we were credited with being the only group to have completed the required dissection for the day.

Thus at any rate ended a most significant year of my life. It was bizarre and macabre but even at this point defined us as those who deal with death and with life.

Anatomy had not been our only course that year. The other courses were academically of no less importance, and biochemistry extremely so. But none had the impact and lasting visual, tactile and olfactory imagery of that studio lab. Today that kind of trauma has passed, as modern students have pre-dissections and computerized images, coddled, one might say.

Neuroanatomy too is over. Here we had spent months on the human brain looking for delicate pathways and nuclei. I and countless others never understood the brain nor its intricate pathways and it is only indeed in recent times as a seasoned attending physician that some of the possibilities of this intricate structure and its complex functions have become meaningful. My survival technique was to construct schematic diagrams to describe nebulous structural relationships. These were like chemical flow diagrams and were designed to pass examinations without understanding the actual brain. My intricate and complex schema applied, in fact, to an entirely fictitious brain. I had never successfully dissected out a single pathway, nor did I have any real concept of how the brain worked.

A landmark year has passed by perhaps the most significant year of my life. I am maturing. I am hardly longer a boy. I feel a veteran. As bizarre and difficult and taxing as the experience has been, in retrospect, my final year of high school was worse. For there, all depended on my final grade and though an exemplary student, a bad day on a single exam would have precluded a medical career. That was a form of psychological torture. To make matters worse, that final year was grade thirteen, not grade twelve, for Ontario schools had this peculiarity of a first college year in high school. While Americans were in universities (as were Quebeckers), we in Ontario were stunted high school collegians except the rich who went off to American universities after grade twelve and returned to start Canadian university, occasionally getting into the second year if their grades were good. Ontario discriminated against its own students.

Medical school also employed a quota system and Jewish boys had to have very high grades for admission. No EOE for Jewish boys and girls. Not in Canada. Not at University of Toronto.

Those were the days, all gone now, or are they....

Our first year had ended, and there were no suicides. One classmate, a young woman whom I had never even spoken to in our class of one hundred and forty students had had a "nervous breakdown", but she did not really count as a medical school casualty, since she departed to hospital at the end of Premeds. She was a dark, shy girl who never said much and bit her fingernails a lot. Rachel Bane also left to get married. She was a high school classmate. And of course there was Byron, now ready to enter Law, which he later referred to as his "second mistake," though he completes it, is successful and becomes an esteemed law professor accruing in girth even as he increased in stature.

I have returned my box of bones. Ugh, am I glad to get rid of that. No longer is it under my bed. This box of bones had never been properly cleaned so some dead flesh still clung. The best use for these bones was demonstrated by a classmate whom I saw hailing a cab by waving a femur vigorously in the air. I kept my skull for awhile. That cost sixteen dollars, and I did opine, a medical student should have a skull of his own.

We are ready for our second year, and I understand we will even be seeing some real live patients.

10

Gord Takes Pity

How can I still be a virgin? How old am I now? Twenty one? I have such desires, brooding and voluptuous that drive me. And yet, here I am. I am a nice guy. Not really. I want to rip their clothes off, even beat them, well, at least whip them, but all I can do is be a gentleman. I am too shy. I am going blind. I spent the summer in New York getting better contact lenses but they are no go. I will need an operation. Next summer, I must demand an operation.

I can't go on like this. I make out with girls but have no steady. These Toronto girls! How they smile. They want to marry me. They want to marry a doctor. But they won't fuck unless I promise. Not the Jewish ones that's for sure, at least not me. There must be some..... Geez how about that Ettie or Gladys Bubbles—but not for me. I dated this Israeli girl who Larry told me liked oral sex. I called her up sight unseen, and told her I met her at a party. When I came to her door, she said, "I never saw you in my life." But she went with me and damn it, she liked me. God, she kissed like a printing press and was amused at how surprised I was at her technique. But I blew it, and that means she didn't. She also wanted to marry me and would not give herself with that in mind since good (Jewish) girls were not supposed to. What could I do? Tell her, "I know you put out. That's why I am dating you, you sexy big titted round assed little bitch!"

Oh, if only I had a car. I had one as a child and now I can't see well enough to drive and have no money even if I could. I continue to see Sabrina quite a few times, over the years off and on, but she never waivers. That is Toronto—even if they did it, they wouldn't and especially not for me. They get insulted if I try to make a date for tomorrow, or even if I call Wednesday for Saturday, since you have to call a full week in advance: "Oh, I really shouldn't go out with you, you naughty boy. Maybe this time I will. Next time, you call a week in advance!" or,

"Oh, I didn't hear from you for so long. I'm sorry, I'm engaged now. You should have called me. Yes, I'm a contented cow." (Susan Finkle with humongous tits!) Whew.

At any rate, it is time for something. I mean it is sex or suicide. Fortunately, my friend Gord, an engineer and a revolutionary socialist, sees that things have reached the brink of desperation, and takes measures. Now Gord has been my buddy since grade nine. He is like a brother but is mildly disreputable, and rather unkempt besides and at times unreliable. For instance, he had left Shendy and me waiting for him in a parking lot while he went to check out a hot party on campus. He knew the guys running it and it promised to be an orgy. Well it was an orgy. In fact, it was so good that Gord never came back for us and we ruefully and frustrated returned home unconsummated and unfulfilled. Next day, Gord showed up at my place.

"Hey, you guys ought to have been there. These two guys took out their dicks and stuck them in the faces of these two broads and they just stared at it! Ha! Ha! And then....."

"You unreliable bastard!" I shriek at him. He is sensitive; he will make it up.

Gord drops over. "C'mon, I got something for yuh!" In the car is sitting Louie Lightstick, a former high school classmate and a rather strange character who is prone to asking profound questions, like "What is Medicine? What Is Psychiatry? Where is Heaven?" If one is so stupid to try to answer these PhD dissertation questions, one observes that Louie is not interested in the answer, only in the question. Apparently asking broad philosophical questions is a measure of one's profundity. I, as a medical student, am regarded as a type of seer in the world of two bit philosophy.

At any rate, there is Louie in the car and another young man whom I have not previously met, an engineering student like Gord and as I learn, a part-time pimp. His name is Philip.

The three of us drive downtown and Philip runs into a small house returning with a very attractive young girl named Brenda.

Apparently she is even Jewish. Like, Wow! She is a succulent thing aged seventeen, with very large breasts that strain at her shirt blouse and jiggle as she has no bra, an unusual thing for these days. My mouth waters at the sight and I cannot take my eyes off her nor believe that I am actually going to get a piece of this. I have attended strip shows since age fifteen, and was always disappointed that the women were not very young and were too professional. Even Gladys was too professional. But this girl seems just ripe. We then pick up another tart, a redhead, also pretty though not as stacked as Brenda.

We arrive at a house in a fairly well-to-do section of the city where the host and quite a few other boys are waiting.

"Well, who do you want?" asks Gord and smiles as I point to the demure Brenda. He had seen me drooling over her, and noted my surprise at the high quality of the offering. Again, this was a Jewish girl though her friend Carole was not. It seems the Jewish girls were totally unattainable or total tarts.

I have to wait my turn in these proceedings. Louie supersedes me, we go in alphabetical order or some such. Finally, after an interminable time, after some coaxing with knocking on the door, Louie appears and saunters down the stairs, his clothes neat and he is twirling an umbrella.

"Greetings, what's your hurry boys?" he queries.

Finally, it is my turn and I ascend the stairs. As I enter the room (apparently our host's parents' room, they are away for the weekend), there stands Brenda naked. Her breasts are huge and perfectly shaped but sad to relate, there is no shock of a big dark bush that I so long to see. Curses, she has shaved and plucked herself. What a disappointment! Moreover, Philip is in the room and he and Brenda are negotiating what payoff to give their host this evening, finally agreeing a free blowjob would be fair for use of his parents' place.

Then Philip departs and Brenda smiles, bades me undress and asks for five dollars.

I proffer this and she proffers a rubber condom.

For all my ravenous desire, the situation is considerably less of a turn on than one might have anticipated and it brings to mind Frank's troubles and his advice to let her do it. She seems more than capable at that and proceeds to insert my member into her mouth since the other way with the condom was not producing sufficient success. There is a time limit you see and a lineup of hungry young men outside. Even her astute oral work is not too fruitful as the fact of having a place in line and a slightly used whore bothers me. She advises me not to kiss her and I understand why since she has had a full mouth more than once today already. Also, she requests I not come in her mouth since she has heard that sperm is alkaline and therefore bad for her teeth. I explain that I am a medical student (which impresses her) and suggest that alkaline sperm may actually prevent cavities by, if anything, neutralizing mouth acids. Still the situation is not the very best, and now there is knocking on the door. Since I am restricted from oral foreplay on her mouth and I presume elsewhere, I ask if she would permit me to suck her (huge) tits. She hesitates at this strange fetish, then assents, which does oddly have a proper result and I bang her fairly solidly to the extent that I fear my contact lenses will fall out. They don't however and the mission is accomplished at least credibly. I am no longer a virgin! There is much knocking at the door as the next shift is ready. I am congratulated, tired and no longer, thank God, a virgin. I hope it will be better next time though. I have to keep doing it till I get it right. How strange and silly it all is in the light of sobriety.

There is some gossip as we wait for another shift or two to finish. The redhead makes googoo eyes at me and says she likes my name. But I have no more money and am through being tested for this time. I hope Brenda doesn't get any more cavities. I am told her father will only let her go out with Jewish boys. A gentile tried to date her and her daddy chased him with a stick but Philip, the pimp (a Jew) is apparently acceptable as is most of the clientele tonight.

11

Hurrah for Hollywood

The train is moving rapidly through the night, oscillating with a vibration I had initially thought pleasant, but which is now making me seasick. The frequency of the vibrations is long and wave-like as opposed to a car, which vibrates rapidly; I am bored and nauseous, and since I must remove my contact lenses to try and sleep in my seat, I am also blind and further isolated. This is the second night on the train as we head west to Los Angeles. I have not seen my sister there for many years and am on a mercy mission to alleviate my family's morbid fears that my sister is trysting with the Devil in Los Angeles.

The man beside me is crowding me in my seat making things all the more cramped and unpleasant. He is talking now with terrible effervescence after remaining totally mute for half the trip. Now he will not shut up, and he spews forth stunning banalities incessantly. I do not wish him to know about my eye difficulties so I must put my contact lenses in and out surreptitiously, which is difficult since he monitors me. He has a Texas drawl, this skinny man in a gray suit and delivers it in a whiny voice, which in the long haul makes me feel like screaming for him to shut up. Ugh! How polite I am.

At long last the trip is over. The scenery at times has been just beautiful when I can concentrate on it, but my eyes and my worries won't let me. Also, I do not know how Gilda will receive me; she seems to think her family is her enemy, and that I was loved most and therefore I am a Premeds student while her life is ruined.

Los Angeles in many ways is like Toronto as I discern it at age twenty. It is a horizontal rather than a vertical city like New York and has far less impact than the "Apple." It lacks a transportation system, which I regard with incredulity, and after one waits an hour for a bus, a sign says "Welcome Aboard."

I feel there is a forced and insincere friendliness. This is typified by slogans everywhere, like "Stow it, don't throw it." People smile and seem helpful, but I feel a veneer beneath, where there is less concern than in my native city. Toronto is stuffy but there is a poison in American cities and I feel a foreigner. One must remember that I was not well travelled and I was merely reflecting a common Canadian prejudice, which comes from living in the shadow of the U.S. colossus. We are at least morally superior, if so much less powerful. I am shocked that the benches at the bus stops are supplied by Morris Mortuary Establishments, Inc.

My sister has received me better than I expected, and perhaps better than she expected. My cousin's wife however seems very hostile to me, since she seems to be siding with my sister and acting like her protector from me. And since Gilda is receiving me well, Sara's hostility is embarrassing. My cousin is a medical student in his final year. He married Sara when they were seventeen, and got Bulbar Polio in Premeds just when the Salk vaccine was discovered. Now he is pretty badly crippled and has lost entire groups of muscles due to that disease. For instance, he cannot extend his arms since his triceps muscles have vanished. He must let his arms extend by gravity. That is, they must fall open. I discuss with him and Gilda his condition and my eyes.

He avers that we all have a cross to bear, which is a pretty nice metaphor for a Jewish guy.

Although my first reaction to the American way is distaste colored by Canadian chauvinism, I find, as has much of the world, that what at first tastes badly can end by tasting rather pleasant, like olives or perhaps heroin. There is something exotic and intoxicating about all these scurrying people and their moving machines, even if their ideology is a paper mache one. Undulating women in their bouffant hairdos and sprayed on tight pants lasciviously punctuate these thoughts.

My sister lives at the Hollywood Studio Club with the starlets. She is a commercial artist and this residence is for women in the arts. I visit her there and see stunning women everywhere, all inaccessible to me. One is dating Hugh O'Brien, another Frank Sinatra. The latter Jo Morrow, has just been signed for a part generating a flurry of catty remarks concerning her. Another very beautiful girl also got a part and a starlet sitting beside us refers to her as "that lesbian." "Oh, look Gilda, she's waving her ass at us. She must be bending over for your brother." For me would she? Perhaps she is at that!

At the Studio Club, the girls are either light blonde or have jet black hair. They all look the same. In the street I stop a girl thinking it is my sister's roommate at the Studio Club.

She is a stranger-mistaken identity; she thinks I want to pick her up. She looks at me disdainfully.

The uglies at the Studio Club sit at a separate table in the lunchroom. They are referred to as "the uglies." There is clique upon clique and the girls talk as if they are ready to commit homicide against one another. I am an observer. I cannot compete here. Time is too short. One could spend a lot of money on these girls. I am too young, unattractive, penniless, blind even.

My sister takes me along to a modeling school where I am permitted to watch a class in session. A homely girl is advised how not to walk "double-track," and with proper use of makeup is transformed into a striking looking woman. I realize that women can learn how to trap men even when not stunningly beautiful.

At the school is a young, blonde girl with a baby face and quite beautiful.

"Gilda," I plead, "I want her."

"Oh, she wouldn't be interested in you!"

Gilda is later very surprised when a starlet friend, Marianna Hill (who has a TV part) remarks, "Why Gilda, you didn't tell me you have a cute brother!"

I am tongue-tied however since she is too sophisticated. "Oh, she thinks she is so beautiful," says Gilda. She seems cute but rather plain. Later, I see her made up and am stunned by her drop-dead beauty!

My sister knows Playboy model June Wilkinson and I meet her at her apartment. She is my age but is also beyond reach and seems years beyond me. She appears soft and lovely with smooth white skin and sweet British accent. I thought she was hard from her pictures in Playboy. She is also small in stature and delicate although voluptuous and I had thought her a giant.

At last my frustration is so great I cannot bear it. I am relieved that I shall soon be returning to sober Toronto, the untitillating.

Before I go, Gilda takes me to see Sara's father, an ophthalmologist. He is very interested in my eyes and tells me about Dr. Castroviejo in New York.

"He is an artist," he informs me.

"The best ocular surgeon in the world."

Also, he tells me to be sure to marry a girl with good eyes.

So far there's nothing to marry. So now I have yet another thing to worry about as yet unborn offspring.

I leave my sister in the American threshing machine and return to cool Canada and Premeds.

12

New York, New York

My first time in New York. My Heavens, what a city! Is that a man lying in a pile of garbage? Look at the people swarming everywhere. What odd shapes! There is a Betty Boop and her boyfriend two of them dressed in white sailor suits and four feet high. Look at the bridges, the concrete and steel, the skyscrapers. How can one function in a place like this? What stimuli! How can one close it out. Sirens!

I walk up Columbus Avenue. There is a crowd ahead of me surging and milling like an organism. Suddenly, the crowd parts as two police cars arrive on the scene. They, the police, exit the car as I continue my slow approach. Then, of a sudden, a bottle is thrown from a high roof landing with an explosion. Pop, pop, pop; the police have guns drawn and God help me, they are shooting to the top of the roof. A New York scene. I learn the pro-Castro Cubans and the anti-Castro Cubans are having a confrontation. Later, I see on TV the anti-Castros wrecking the HQ of the pro-Castros, filmed by TV. TV is there but no police.

Later, I stop for a hamburger on Broadway, at a street stand.

The hamburger is greasy and drips onto the counter. "Please," I ask the counterman, "a serviette." "Soivie who?" I am asked.

"A serviette" I say. I am left dumb at this inability to be understood. Finally, I say, "Napkin, have you got a napkin?"

I am proffered a napkin and the counterman asks, "Hey, what did youse say? Soiveyet? I neva hoid dat before."

"It's a word," I say.

"Well, I been in restaurants all round New York and I neva hoid dat before. Hey Lou," he asks, "Have you heard deeze called soiveyets?"

Lou is a slow moving, elderly black man with a tired look. "Well, some calls dem dat," he says.

As I finish the greasy hamburger, the counterman is cooking, tossing burgers and shaking his head, "Soiveyet. Soiveyet."

"Well, live and loin, live and loin."

On the subway, I put my coins in the booth and they are pushed back at me, no token and no explanation. I reinsert them to the booth man; they are shoved back. Finally, I reexamine the coins and see a nickel is Canadian. I substitute an American nickel and get a token.

I try to pass a five dollar bill (U.S.) at the subway station; it gets the same treatment. I find the right coins and pass through the turnstile. I wait in the dingy tunnel for a rundown train. I walk along the platform and my way is blocked by a fat little man with a moustache. I step aside, but he steps the same way and we both repeat this doing a rather funny dance. I am slightly amused as we pass each other finally, but he turns and looks back at me and snarls, "Can't you let a guy get by?"

My (3rd) cousin Rebecca is kind to me. She is an attractive older woman who has put me up. She is married to a psychiatrist and has just had a child. I find her vivacious and wish she were my sister. I watch her attractive legs and admire her sophistication. One day, she asks me if I am trying to seduce her. She has seen me watching her legs. I deny it. I am shocked.

"Oh, you are shocked" she says. "Oh, I don't shock easily," I say. "Yes you do," she says.

She is right. It does not quite dawn on me that the question "Are you trying to seduce me?" may be an invitation to do so, for I am too stupid in these matters. Also I am prudish enough to rationalize that I would be betraying a husband, who has also been more than decent to me, too dumb to comprehend that certain exotic behaviors, unthinkable in Toronto, might be the norm in New York.

Such is the innocence of youth.

At night, I hear noises in the street. Out in the heat, I see three figures walking along. One is carrying a sabre I think; it catches the light and glows ominously. I hear a woman shout,

"My purse, my purse!"

"Aren't you afraid of being mugged?" I ask Rebecca. "Not me," she says.

"A young woman was mugged on the doorstep two days ago. They hit her on the head and took her purse". I remind her. She shrugs her shoulders.

I stepped over a woman in the street last night; a man was beating her up. It looked like a family fight.

It's time to leave. Time to go back to school. I, who am desperately sexually frustrated, searching for a piece of something have passed up another opportunity. Am I a fool, then?

13

The Autopsy; Tale of a Lily Liver

I have returned from strange adventures in New York. That world and the one I inhabit seem so disparate that one or the other cannot be real. In America, while I was there, there was a most serious confrontation between Kennedy and Khrushchev, and for a while, I thought that neither my travail with eyes nor medical school would soon be of any consequence, for it seemed we were heading for a holocaust. That was the Cuban missile crisis. In New York for a few days there was an air of hysteria, and I had been witness and truly petrified. Kennedy seems to have come out of it a hero, but while I was in New York, I thought he might plunge us into war at any moment. The shrill and jingoistic newscasts were terrifying. "They will strike here first," I thought. How ironic, a short visit to New York and I will go up in a puff of smoke.

The year has recommenced. I have new contact lenses fitted painfully in New York. I have scleral as well as standard corneal lenses. This permits me to vary my study habits by alternating different lenses and things are a little easier. The second year is more relaxed than the first, which was so grueling. As I have indicated, high school was really more demanding intellectually. Medicine, especially the first year, was just hard work, with voluminous material to cover, mostly to commit to memory, without analysis or critical evaluation.

As Anatomy had been the major subject last year, Pathology is the big subject this year. It is considerably more interesting, however, since it is based on clinical material, that is to say actual people.

Today, I am to attend my first autopsy. Dr. Macduff, another droll Scotsman, is lecturer and demonstrator in this course. He has a dark sense of humor and never fails to get a laugh from the young second year students. A lecture on the male reproductive system would begin: "Well, as you all know, the male scrotum is a sack containing all sorts of odds and ends...."

Since much of the material had to do with ways of dying, this allowed for an expected modicum of gallows humor, which at times was geared to shock a naive audience, and naive we still were, having only just emerged from the insulated if grim cocoon of the first year, and not as yet having met a patient.

I enter a strange amphitheater and I sit on a hard backless bench. The room is dim and there is a light on stage where Dr. Macduff is chatting animatedly to his three volunteers for this auspicious occasion, which thank God did not include me and I would have in any case gone to great lengths to avoid this "first." I needn't have worried for there are always keen students in class, ready to show how calm and efficient and able they are. It is not hard therefore for me to fade into the background and keep my profile low. There are two males and a female volunteering for this and there are some twenty of us in the bleachers. I have not chosen a ringside seat though my view is all too good.

Dr. Macduff, seeing the initiates have gathered, gives a signal to an assistant, an aide-orderly-ghoul who wheels in a stretcher.

This, mark you, is the very first hot body. Not a cadaver, and not an aged relative in a funeral casket. This was a living breathing human being only a few hours earlier. Why rigor mortis has barely set in! I am hoping it will be someone old; someone who has died timely and properly. But it is not. Not hardly! The cover is pulled back to reveal, my God, a young red haired woman, no more than twenty-two, twenty-three years old. All naked stiff and warm. Oh, she was beautiful. A girl you would want to date, to have. She had a bush too, a beautiful red bush. Oh, My God! Luscious. But dead, so dead. I was shocked as were my cohorts. There was a communal gasp then total silence.

I feel slightly nauseous. And Macduff cracks some gallows joke. Ugh! Get me out of here. I want to run, to cry but I cannot move. Heavens, I have this thing about death, you see.... The others are faring no better. Is it the dark or is Ken's face green? There is dead silence. The poor beautiful young red headed woman had died three hours earlier (I am hearing) of heart failure due to rheumatic heart disease. We will therefore take a look at the heart in question. Hail Macduff! I continue to watch in panic with hysteria sweeping over me but I am transfixed and watch in dreadful fascination.

Do you think I should go on with this? It is too dreadful to recall. Macduff takes out this curved knife, see. He sets the poor woman's head on a wooden support block and as he begins an incision the head falls off the block with a dull thud that causes a yelp from several quarters. The body is repositioned and Macduff cuts into the rib cage. There is the grim staccato sound like a train going over a bumpy trestle. He repeats this now on the right side, then lifts the entire chest cage up to open the chest with a terrible CRACK as the sternum is broken. All the while he is making wry remarks to the nervous tittering of the students. Then the Professor incises the heart and removes it for the young-uns to view. He points out its huge size and indicates that a disrupted heart valve from rheumatic fever had caused this leading finally to heart failure ventricular fibrillation and death. He cuts up the heart while the poor woman placidly lies naked and exposed in death. Who was she, this poor young woman? I know not but someone loved her not long ago.

The autopsy is not at end, for one must, I learn, examine other organ systems. The abdomen is sliced and the intestine removed like so much coiled rope. Macduff pulls it out like a sailor making fast a ship. Then he deftly cuts into the liver to remove that, and horror of horrors, a spurt of blood shoots into the air and hits the female volunteer student, who shrieks, "Oh, my eye!" I am unnerved beyond belief yet too frozen to run. The others are the same. None of us is made of steel.

Finally, this weird Macduff cuts the scalp and saws the skull to look at the brain, and a stench the likes of which I have never experienced before, fills the room. Now I cover my mouth and I am really gagging. At last, it is over, the grimmest of the grim experiences and I stagger; I run from the amphitheater, a black joke ringing in my ear like the clunk of a skull smacking against a hard cold slab. How cold it is. I shiver. I am shivering.

Outside in the clear sunlight which rays hurt my eyes, I try to calm myself and seek to be alone.

I attend other autopsies in future experiences, which are laborious events and do not scarcely match this first experience so vividly impressed on a young student struggling to cope with the realities of life and death.

14

The Eyes Have It

I feel at peace at summer camp. I am seventeen in charge of a cabin of rowdy thirteen year old boys. They are a difficult group and one of them is disturbed and has begun going into the girls' toilets. I am afraid we will have to send him home. He is, poor boy, very aware of girls but unable to develop any sort of a normal relationship. He describes his girlfriend by gesturing with his hands an hourglass figure, but he puts in three loops instead of the customary two to describe upper and lower torso. The other campers laugh. Yesterday, I had to chase him all over the field and restrain him after he bothered a group of girls.

Yet the camp is far away from the worries of school. When I return to Toronto, I will enter grade thirteen, and years of good scholastic work will become meaningless. The university will review only what I attain on the final matriculation examinations. Also, I must attain a very high percentage to get into medical school since there is a quota on those with my ethnic background (a.k.a. Jews). Thus, I must have at least an eighty percent average (seventy-five is first class) while others can enter with a lower average even with sixty to sixty-five percent. I choke at the unfairness but do as the others in this situation, I just put up with it, powerless to change it.

The camp director is Michel Herzog. Oddly, he taught me Hebrew when I was seven. I was his worst student, and while getting A++'s in public school, at Hebrew school at night, I was getting Gimels (alef, beth, gimel). Michel warned me I could fail, but I was quite smart and he knew it. He smiled when I replied, "so you mean I won't have a Bar-Mitzah?" The Bar-Mitvah was of course inevitable for a Jewish boy so failure was impossible even if I tried to fail. My inevitable Bar materialized in fact at thirteen, but of course. I did however, totally memorize the Torah dissertation without understanding a word—a good preliminary for medical training.

I was too young when Michel taught me, and school after hours was not for me. But at Camp Kvutzah he is rather fun. He lets me drive his new Ford, a blue 1956 car. It is the best car I have driven. It is so powerful.

I do not drive a car again for ten years.

I am on lifeguard duty. I am on the pier watching the campers swimming. I have to wait for them to finish before I can take a dip too. I am watching the campers, and also watching Judith Eisner, who is the best female counselor in camp, in charge of a cabin of thirteen year old girls. I have a crush on her, this competent and pretty girl. I was told she liked me, but not knowing what to do, I asked her point blank if the "rumors were true," and she modestly backed away. How awkward I am! Now I look at her in her tight pink bathing suit. She is seventeen years old like me, and has a narrow waist and moderately nice sized tits. Her hips are wide and suddenly flare out and her legs are thin and shapely. She will probably get too fat later in life with such wide hips. But how pretty now! How I would like to put my hands on her firm little body.

I look out over the water. Lately, the glare of the water seems to bother my eyes an awful lot. One shouldn't look at the sun. Perhaps it is hurting my eyes. There seem to be dancing lights. My eyes are bothering me.

Soon the season ends. I am back home and school is due to start in two weeks. I visit Dr. Exner, the family oculist who examines me thoroughly and gives me weaker glasses.

"Your eyes are improving," he tells me.

He carefully looks in my eyes with his ophthalmoscope and seems a little perplexed. Perhaps I will not need glasses, which I have used for mild myopia since grade seven. My nearsightedness has been such that I can read very easily without glasses and I enjoy books therefore, but reading is recently more of a strain. Dr. Exner's glasses do not solve the problem and he prescribes new lenses. This seems ridiculous to me. I am worried about my eyes and worried about medical school.

"Why do you want to go to medical school?" asks the oculist. "Medicine is a rich man's hobby!"

I decide Dr. Exner is too old to continue treating me and he is telling me things are good when I see they are not. I do not like his advice either!

Having no money, I go to Northeast General Hospital to the eye clinic. A young attending in ophthalmology examines me, first casually, then with interest. Finally, he calls over a physician passing by. "Hey, look at this," he calls. He is visibly excited. The other physician looks into my eyes through a slit lamp. "See the shadows," says the first. "What an interesting case!"

They have forgotten I am a person. I am an "interesting case". Then the first doctor turns to me.

"Young man, you have an interesting condition. It is very early keratoconus. You have a defect in the surface of your eye, a thinning of the cornea, and that is creating astigmatism. This will probably slowly get worse, but at some point, contact lenses could help."

I have been diagnosed. I have been briefed. I have been convicted and condemned. What will become of me? Can I go to medical school? Can I get through grade thirteen? I am decimated.

15

The First Patient

In the second half of the second year, we begin to learn about patients. Dr. Hicks is an endocrinologist and we are on rotation through St. Michael's, a very good small hospital in Toronto, a Catholic institution.

Dr. Hicks explains the fundamentals of a physical examination, and describes how to do a neurological. He will show us on real patients and he does. One man, a stroke victim, displays the Babinsky Reflex; Dr. Hicks scrapes the bottom of his foot with a tongue depressor and the toes curl up instead of down.

I go home and run a tongue depressor around the sole of my foot. Oh God, it's curling up. I have a Babinsky!

On Monday, I anxiously relay my horrible neurological finding to Dr. Hicks. I have been very worried over the weekend.

"Look," I say, "there is something neurologically wrong with me. I have a Babinsky."

Dr. Hicks does not appear worried. In fact, he laughs. "Are you walking around?"

"Well uh, yes." "Then you don't have a Babinsky. If you are paralyzed, you can't walk around, see."

I am relieved and laugh too with my classmate group though still slightly worried. Slightly red faced too, truth to say.

A new patient of Dr. Hicks has just been admitted. Ken and I will examine him and present him. He is our first case. He is a friendly fifteen year old boy, who is perfectly well, who is admitted on a research project since he has an unusual genetic condition: Klinefelter's Syndrome. This is an XXY genetic makeup rather than a normal XY. He is a little retarded but is amicable and happy, as Kenny and I examine him. He has breasts and is hairless on his body and he has small genitals. He is not quite male or female, poor soul. But he does not seem unduly bothered by this. We report on him and talk about him and I follow his course for the next few days.

The weekend comes and goes. It is Monday and we return to the ward. My patient's bed is empty.

"Where is Donny? I ask the nurse. She evades me. Then the head nurse comes in.

"Donny has died," she says.

"My God, there was nothing wrong with him! He was here for research follow-up!"

"He died of staph pneumonia," she replies dryly. "It happens." Shaken, I leave the ward. I meet Kenny just coming in.

"Donny is dead." I say with awe. "Our first patient is dead."

16

Trotsky Lives

"Hey, you are persona non grata around here."

She says this with a friendly fixed smile, this girl with the round wire rimmed glasses and plain face devoid of makeup. Katrina is an unstable young woman whom most of us avoid and I know her fairly well through her brother. She has recently had a breakdown and was hearing voices and screaming but now she is okay. So a non compos mentis is telling me I am persona non grata. Do you think I care? You are all crazy.

Gord has taken pains with me to get me to come to a few of these meetings at the bookstore over the years but I have stood apart so am now persona non grata. Why, Katrina's brother was even arrested two months ago and spent the night in jail! Some kind of battle on a picket line. A great honor, was it a ban-the-bomb rally? Those were run by a pseudo-leftist who is later caught in a scandal. Seems he had used his university buyer's job to outfit several boarding houses he had purchased by some finagling. At any rate, I have never been in jail, though my few appearances at the bookstore may well have put my photo into the RCMP file of radicals.

I regret to say that I view the Movement as a joke and have succumbed to Gord's persuasion as much in the quest for ass as in hopes of bringing in a new world order. Sadly, I have found little ass at least to this point. I do befriend several young men however.

They all seem to be engineers like Gord so I gather he has been doing some recruiting. There is Hans, who is a handsome Aryan youth. He is intelligent and sensible, I wonder what he is doing here perhaps expiating Nazi sins? And I befriend a Japanese man several years older than myself whom I find interesting and intense. He had left Japan after the war, deeply disillusioned with his society. The generals had lied to the people. The Emperor was a man, not a God. Sumi had actually volunteered to become a Kamikaze pilot and would have died as did many compatriots and classmates in a raging inferno for the Emperor. He was too young for this by one year and was crushed that he could not be a part of such glory. When he learned of the lies of Imperial Japan, he was psychologically shattered.

For a year, he wandered aimlessly around the countryside of his homeland and finally collected himself, applied for a visa to Canada and left Japan forever.

Gord's girlfriend is Lillian. She is a pretty Scottish girl with flaming red hair, who is a staunch politico. She is short but well built and pretty but also kind of crazy. She is rather fanatical I think. One night, she tells me her story, her misgivings, her hard and poor upbringing and lack of education, how the Movement has educated her, how she has needed something.

She was a Salvation Army worker before, but that was not enough. Nothing was until she found this.

The leader of the cell is Ross Dawson, a balding man in his forties. He is a perennial losing candidate for mayor. Talking to him is like talking to a political encyclopedia. What he says makes sense, but he says it so assertively, so certainly, in such flat tones, that I am repelled. Also I realize that Canada is too small for a great revolution, too tied to the U.S. and not by any means troubled enough. The Movement is insular, cut off from the masses who might sympathize with it. The masses are in fact, persona non grata. The 'cell's' mistrust leads to an inbreeding and isolation, which has turned the participants into a quixotic movement, comprising an inordinate number of identitiless, searching, semi-psychotics, or others trying to find some purpose for empty lives. Further some of them, for all I know maybe all, are agents, RCMP, spying on each other.

One man named Harold Silver is actually retarded and seems to be the Movement's mascot, hanging around, making funny sounds and gestures. Some of the people, however, are decent, perceptive and intelligent.

"Have you seen those two volumes of Das Kapital?" I ask my mother. She hasn't seen them. "What, all my leftist literature is gone! Geez, it's Gord's, not even mine! Where is the box of books?"

Finally a confession. She threw them all out. How am I going to explain this? Just the way she got rid of Soviet Life. My poor dad had bought a year's subscription to that. Censorship.

She had me laughing at my father for his "red" ties. All Soviet Life had in it were couples in tractors, riding off into the sunset to a factory somewhere near the Volga. The Militant also appeared at times too and was promptly burned in the coal furnace when we had coal and shredded when we converted to oil.

Now Gord's collection on loan to me has met the same fate.

That's what happened to a hardback of Forever Amber too. Well, I still read Playboy. Mother saved me from the RCMP or even the FBI, I guess.

I almost became a Trotskyist for ass. Perhaps If I had got some, I would have been a revolutionary.

17

A Bad Omen

Second Meds has gone by rapidly. It has been a difficult year, even in some respects worse than last year. My eyes are greatly bothering me and the scleral contact lenses make my corneas edematous after I use them so the smaller lenses do not work well either. The small lenses continue to pop out of my eyes onto the ground, at times to be found after a lengthy search, embedded in one's shoe.

Pathology, which has its good moments, is nonetheless a considerable problem for me, particularly histopathology requiring extensive use of the microscope. Thus, as the end of the year rolls around, I am exhausted and practically hysterical. My eye problem precludes long hours of study and after putting in two or three hours at the books, I telephone Kenny for reassurance only to hear him exhaustedly exclaim that he has been studying intensively for nine straight hours and is literally nauseated and gagging. I hang up more panicked than ever. There is no reassurance. I believe I will fail—the Pathology practical consisting of more than half microscopic work. I am sure will be a disaster, and when I confront this exam, I am not far wrong.

This will be the last year I shall spend in such agony, I am resolved.

On the practical, I see my contact lenses in the microscope and am sure I am describing those. This is worse than the days of histology for we are expected to know more and make conclusions rapidly and I can barely get focused before we must move to the next specimen.

In view of my difficulties, I have the conviction I will fail despite a good B standing the previous year and a similar average this year so far. I ask Dr. Kanan, my ophthalmologist for a letter to the Dean of Medicine explaining my plight and requesting consideration should I not succeed. Fortunately, I do succeed since the year's work counts for something and I make B standing once again, to my great surprise. I feel silly having sent my letter, and happy that I made it on my own. My sense of foreboding had been so great and even now I feel I will somehow not make it through. The droll autopsy is etched in my mind as is Professor Duckworth's dire prediction. Will one of us die?

Will I? Sometimes I fantasize collapsing on a grueling practical, with people rushing to look after me. I want to be cared for. To be pitied. To be loved. Oh, how miserable I am.

In one of our last classes of the year, I learn that an honor student a year ahead of us has died. He was a French professor's son. Some say he died in a skiing accident, but those in the know say he took his own life.

18

O Say Can I See

Now I am on a slab. I am like a cadaver waiting to be dissected. I stare at the bright light above me shining at me. I am transfixed by these events in an altered state of consciousness. Though exquisitely aware of everything around me, I am totally immobile and detached from my person.

I am back in New York. I am on an operating table and in moments Dr. Ramon Castroviejo, the world's foremost ocular surgeon, in fact, literally the Picasso of eye surgery, will perform surgery on my right eye. It will be a corneal transplant. Someone else's cornea will be put into my eye and my own cornea removed. My cornea, the transparent covering of the eye, is not spherical and after five years of dependence on contact lenses and impaired vision, I have had enough, and Dr. Castroviejo has agreed to operate. The operation will be very costly and I will be unable to work this summer. I will have to get a loan to continue school. Dr. Castroviejo assures me there is a very high likelihood of success for this operation, about ninety-five percent he has said. That still leaves a five percent risk and a variable outcome possible. But I am young, healthy and my eye condition, though a handicap, is not a severe condition, being at an early stage in its course. The operation, if successful, will be fully curative.

Now I am on the table overtaken by events, and waiting breathlessly for my turn. There have already been several operations today; mine is the fourth. Apparently, twelve or thirteen are performed by this incredibly skilled surgeon in one day, three days per week.

As I lie on the table in a state of some form of hypnosis, I try to comprehend what is happening. When I was wheeled into the room, in a wheelchair, there were, I perceived with my blurred but intact vision, three operating tables in the room. Unexpectedly, the doctors are busy at one of the tables and there are movie floodlights. They are operating on someone and filming it. There are voices in Spanish and in English and there is some laughing and joking. I am stunned with this situation, and also by the fact that I am fully conscious where I had assumed I would be receiving a general anesthetic. They have given me one Trancopal preop (a mild tranquilizer) and nothing else.

While the proceedings with the other patient continue, I am instructed to lie quietly. I lie, thankful I can do so, otherwise I should certainly collapse.

In due course, someone approaches me from behind, and while the activity at the other end of the room to my left is unabated, I suddenly am injected in my face with a needle. My lower face on the right side promptly becomes numb, in fact paralyzed by local anesthesia. Then a needle passes over my eye and sticks below my right eyebrow. I flinch with the sharp pain and then again and then again as the facial nerve is blocked in all its branches sensory and motor. Now my face on the right is totally paralyzed. Then a type of retractor is placed into my eye to push back the now flaccid lids and I am draped, shutting off my left eye from events but leaving the right eye exposed and peculiarly watching the action. This is a weird state of affairs. I must impress the fact that my ocular problem was astigmatism, like looking out of a window where the glass, though clear, is imperfect; therefore although I cannot make out fine details, I am yet able to follow events quite well with this eye. It is literally watching itself being operated upon.

Now as the other operation is winding up, and as I stare at the bright sun of the overhead OR light, a hand passes over my eye with something in it. Then I perceive a drop of liquid falling on my cornea and then another and another. I am nearsighted too, I might add, so I can see things very close to the eye itself. I used to be pleased at this since it enabled me to read with great ease and without glasses in the old days before my trouble. My mild myopia was like having a built in magnifying glass. Thus I can see these droplets literally hitting the surface of my eye. It is like someone within me watching the front surface of my eye, rather like being underwater and looking at the still surface of the water above you and someone is throwing pebbles into it.

Now they have wheeled the other patient out of the room. The group has moved to me. Something is put to my eye.

"Can you feel this?" asks a voice. I feel some pressure. A few more drops. Then there is laughing and joking in Spanish. A voice says, "OK, go ahead."

They are not talking to me; I am a specimen.

"That one was for the camera" says a voice, "This one is for the audience."

More laughing. Then, "go ahead."

An instrument hovers in the air over my eye, then descends; it is a marking stylus and I comprehend from the conversation, wielded, to my dismay, by some sort of student.

"No, that's not right." says a voice. "Look, do it this way."

Again the stylus descends to my eye. My God, they are engraving my eye!

As I watch the bright overhead light burning into my soul, I see a scalpel descending down on me. It moves away again.

"You are looking too far to the right. Move your eye to the left," instructs a mildly accented voice.

Ye Gods! They think this is a haircut. I had thought the eye muscles were anesthetized at least! Again the scalpel descends down to my poor eye and now it is cutting into my very eye. As the scalpel moves along the perimeter of the surface of the eye, of the cornea, suddenly all goes dark. The terrible intensity of the OR light is gone. It is no longer a burning sun. But in this darkest blackness, I see far overhead the cool glow of the distant moon, my vision without a cornea. I am exposed and vulnerable. The top of my eye is cut off, and the eyeball is sitting there with its insides open to the elements, just like a soft-boiled egg. If I sneeze now or even move, I shall be blind forever. Suddenly, something is slapped over my naked eyeball and the lights come on again. But now the glass is frosted and I can perceive only light with no vision. Then I am being sewed and sewed. At one point, I do something perhaps I try to blink and I am sharply admonished.

"Stop that, I cannot go on if you do that." I try to keep stiller than ever. I am too conscious, too able to move, too able to get up and walk away.

Finally, a bandage is slapped over my eye tightly and all is dark. The drapes are removed and I am told to sit up, then to get into a wheelchair. I am wheeled out of the room and the doctors and observers have already lost interest in me and have moved to the freshly occupied far table again. I am on an assembly line.

Pajamaed specimens are wheeled upright and scared to the operating theater, deposited on a table for no more than forty minutes and summarily wheeled away again, now with a black patch on one eye. The procedure took thirty-five minutes for me. Recovery would take nine weeks.

My right eye had been operated on this summer; next summer, it would be my left.

19

But Can He Sing Soprano?

I have been deposited in my semi-private room. My right eye is bandaged pirate style and as I am not permitted to wear my left contact lens for fear of 'sympathetic irritation' in the operated eye. Though I can make out blurred forms, I am virtually blind. I have a roommate and there are visitors who laugh and talk and smoke cigars. I am nauseous and this intensifies with the revelry.

For a while, I lie stunned at the events that just transpired. In due course, feeling begins to return to the right side of my face and with it intense agonizing pain in my right eye. My eye feels as though something is in it sticking me and this is accentuated when I try to blink it or otherwise move it.

I cry for pain killers and get codeine, which paralyses but does not relieve the pain. Darvon likewise seems to do little for the pain though I find I am so high on this that I am flying and the pain almost doesn't matter. Finally I discover that two aspirin are best and these relieve the pain for four hours exactly and then like Cinderella's pumpkin, the pain returns with a vengeance and I cry for more aspirin. I am at the mercy of the nurses for this until my dutiful mother begins smuggling aspirin to me.

My mother attends me. She has made her first flight to New York to look after me. She seems to be feeling my pain.

A young woman friend Lee visits me also and for a few moments breaks my despair. She was a child when we met at camp and we have had a brother-sister relationship for some years. She is poetic and sensitive, or plays at this and charms me. She has written me flowery and romantic letters. But she flits like a little fairy, a tinker bell who soon flies off and I am more alone than ever.

At times, I feel I am a Christ figure. I have nails in me only in a different place (at least one in my eye). My suffering is surely worse even than that suffering Jewish deity, I am thinking. I see some people regard me as a tragic hero or as a beautiful figure and I play into this. The beauty of pain. Am I beautiful? No! No! I am deformed, ugly, useless, I am spoiled goods. Will I die even like a Jesus on the cross?

Will I be blind? They cut into me! My eye was a soft boiled egg. Would you like yours poached? Wasn't there an eye in the soup in Cancer Ward? Was it mine? Don't the Arabs eat the eyes of sheep? Don't the Oriental Jews? Doesn't that give you Tay Sachs Disease?

I wince as I see my mother. She is suffering, suffering for me. She is in more pain than I and matches groan for groan.

She is always there. I worry for her this mystical other universe twin who falls when I am struck. And yet thank goodness she is here for I should die of isolation and loneliness if I must endure this trial alone.

I am slipping into a deep depression. I am eating virtually nothing and my weight is falling. The nurses chide me and try to withhold aspirin. "Do you want an ulcer?" I angrily demand my medication. I cannot worry for ulcers when I have my eyes to worry about now!

At the hospital there is much hope and much despair. Dr. Castroviejo is a great surgeon, the greatest, in fact. But even he cannot perform magic. Some eyes are too scarred or damaged and repair can only be palliative. There is a peculiar relationship between the eye and the genitals for the cut eye makes one feel a trauma below too—a castration. A young man becomes an exhibitionist and is summarily transferred to another facility. The small private hospital cannot tolerate this behavior and yet it is not surprising. There is no counseling, no one to offer support, no reassurance. Some will see, some will not.

My own chances are very good. I am young and my condition was a limited one. My own tissue had no scarring, it was just slightly thinned. My likelihood of success is 95% I am told and yet now I see nothing, just the blurred world of my left eye and I am afraid.

Dr. Castroviejo makes rounds from time to time. "Put away your razor," a young attending doctor whispers as I am shaving electrically in Braille, "He is coming." Dr. Castroviejo enters with a retinue of nurses and doctors. He nods and moves on. He is like a king, this man of stocky physical and gigantic medical stature. There is scurrying preceding him and in his wake. An elderly lady kisses his hand in gratitude. Good Lord, what reverence! Will I ever command anything like that esteem? I am a doctor too or soon to be. I can never be a surgeon though, not with these eyes. Will I ever be a doctor at all? Will I see?

A discussion about Cuba with a former WWII flyer ends in an argument. A good American can see nothing good in Cuba under Castro. "Hey, even the Reader's Digest was pro-Castro until he started nationalizing a few things! Battista was a killer, wasn't he? You mean, he was better than Castro? Didn't the Vancouver Sun say that no children are starving in Cuba?"

"That pinko." I hear the elderly night nurses asking if the kid in room 110 is a commie. Better not talk about Castro anymore in the U.S.

"Hey, whatcha' doin?" Nurse Bryant pulls the blankets off me as I lay hot and thrashing. That horny old bitch. She thought I was naked 'cause I had my top off. She's disappointed. Ugh! Thank God I have something on. Aren't there any pretty girls for me?

I sweat and I itch. A rash breaks out and I have a fever. Is it infection? Will I lose my eye after all? No, the mild tranquilizer (Trancopal) I have been getting regularly has produced an allergic reaction. It is stopped as it was an unnecessary routine, I feel much better. My wool blanket causes sneezing and also must go. I am allergic to everything. I am not to sneeze! I am not even allowed to be constipated for any strain builds up pressure on the eye. Magnesia and cascara are an explosive solution like TNT and leave me enervated, exhausted, a biological organism, but hardly a person.

20

Long John Silver

Three exhausting weeks have gone by. Three weeks of blindness. I am to be discharged from the hospital now, but the ordeal, though lessened, is far from over. For still I cannot see and my eye will remain bandaged for six more weeks. The stitches however are removed, thirty in all, and I am tremendously relieved as the pain diminishes. Even the stitch removal is an ordeal, accomplished by assistants to the eminent doctor in almost the time taken for the initial surgery. I am out finally. The pain is vastly less and I hobble in the street. My danger, if anything, has increased however, for now I must not strain at all for fear of increasing intraocular pressure and harming the graft. A bad cold could do me great harm at this point.

My mother and I, on meager funds, retire to a one room residence hotel on the West side. We have a hot plate and no air conditioning and the air, with windows open, is like an oven.

We both suffer and I fear, she more than I. It is 90-95º at night. We hear the noises of the street at night and my mother describes the activities in the lively, cheap but semi-decent hotel across the street, much like our own. "Oh, there is a man beating his wife. Oh, there are naked people dancing together shame, shame. Two men yet." Toronto was never like this. And the hot tropical air makes breathing a great chore.

In the day, we walk to Riverside Park. I, through the blur of my left eye, see a little boy peering at me. Children are frightened by my bandage and black patch.

I try to make a phone call. The operator tells me to dial. "I can't," I say, with some satisfaction for I am entitled to sympathy. "I'm blind."

"Sir, you didn't tell me that. How am I supposed to know you're blind? In the future, say so in the beginning."

A lecture. New Yorkers are not so sympathetic to the disabled. I once saw an awful argument between a cripple and a bus driver. The crippled man was threatening to knock the driver's block off and the whole bus was tittering with amusement. New Yorkers don't seem to ask for sympathy either. They ask no quarter and surely give none.

I sit on a hill overlooking the Hudson River. The breeze is softer here and I have been given a gift of a sixteen dollar transistor radio, one of the first and I play with this toy.

At dusk, the white people depart and the park is filled with young, black men and women putting out blankets and breaking out bottles of liquor in paper bags. Some start to neck heavily on the blankets. In the deep night, goodness only knows what goes on, for the city's population is like a forest of animals who prey, some by night and some by day.

I shunt back and forth to the hospital on ramshackle, crosstown buses, which jar me, so I fear for my operation. The bandages are changed. Lights peer into the operated eye. Drops are put in, and then I am re-bandaged. Things are a blur and I cannot tell If I will see, if it will be any better than it was.

Finally, after nine weeks, the bandages come off for good. For the last week or so, it was just some tissue over the eye anyway.

The eye is refracted and glasses fitted. As the appropriate glass is adjusted, I can see! I am very nearsighted, but with glasses have 20/20 vision. A beautiful result. I have a beautiful diamond shaped graft, which I can just make out in the mirror and I can see well. There will be mild residual astigmatism but contact lenses for my right eye will never again be necessary. In fact, if I wish, I can wear contact lenses with no more problems than anyone else for my cornea now has a proper spherical rather than cone shape on which the contact lenses would sit and not fall out as previously. I have however, no desire to try that out.

Now we are departing from the residence hotel. We say goodbye to the proprietress, a helpful woman who sadly has an ailing heart. As I leave the hotel with my mother, we both exhausted by our ordeal, the proprietress' nephew, recently returned from abroad, rushes over to take the suitcase from my mother. He scolds me for letting her carry the suitcase, unaware as he is of my operation. My mother explains that I must not strain for awhile longer that her son has just had an eye operation. He becomes subdued but still looks sullen. New Yorkers are never wrong no matter what. He gruffly puts the suitcase into a cab and a surly and silent cab driver takes us to the airport.

A letter from the proprietress' sister some weeks later informs us that the woman has died. She has left her eyes to the New York eye bank.

21

Real Patients

It is September and I am back at school now. I am now wearing glasses though what this means is I cannot see on my left side, since the contact lens and glasses do not go well together. I am now more relaxed however, for my vision in the right eye is reasonable despite this difficulty.

The days are cooler and the leaves are falling. A cold winter will soon be upon us, and I will be tramping on hard snow that crunches underfoot, and the cold air will make my nose stick when I breathe it in. Toronto is not so cold as Montreal, nor not nearly so cold as Winnipeg, but the icy winds blowing off Lake Ontario make one impatiently await the warm spring. February, at which the last fury of winter is hurled, is known as the suicide month and from March on, there is an uplifting feeling till the fall. But now we are bracing ourselves.

This is the start of the clinical years in medicine. It is now that we employ the principles of physical examination that we touched on last year, and we spend most of our time examining real patients. We are also to look over treatment and make diagnoses as well. We present cases regularly at the bedside, and are schooled in bedside manners. We do not say "syphilis" near a patient, but rather, "lues," a euphemism a.k.a. code word! Likewise, we never mention "cancer" or "CA," not even "metastatic disease." We talk of "Mitotic disease"(unnatural cell division). Often, we slip up or screw up or a patient mishears and fears for his life.

We are very young and some patients regard us as a nuisance and a penalty for public care (pre OHIP/National Medicine).

Nurses also regard us as a nuisance—the older ones that is. The younger ones don't seem to mind us. I start dating nurses. I am not really aware at this point of the male-female battleground between doctors and nurses as portrayed in Cuckoo's Nest or Intern Dr. X., but it is there, the eternal battle between men and women (a small crossover of female doctors notwithstanding).

I am assigned to a relatively young male patient. I look over his chart and see he has Hodgkin's Disease. What a shame! He is around 30, and got ill just a short time ago. As I approach his bedside, he groans, "Oh no, not again!" He has been examined by many students. I talk with him a little while and am sympathetic. He responds to a little kindness and I conduct a physical examination as I am supposed to. His spleen is very enlarged according to the chart and I search for it. I am not sure I am feeling spleen. I guess I am. I percuss as I am told to do, and hear a duller sound like there is something there.

He has prominent lymph nodes under his arms and in his groin.

He tells me he has a five year old daughter. What will become of his family? He is near tears. I return to see him a number of times. He seems to be improving. One day, I find there is someone else in his bed. I learn that he suddenly expired two days ago. I am sad and a helpless feeling overwhelms me.

On the wards, I examine a woman in her fifties. I am becoming more experienced and am acutely aware of female modesty, especially in older women—who though they greet me with forbearance—bite their lips and endure great pains in this indignity. This lady, however, is not too modest. Moreover, she is cracking lewd jokes and will not let me drape her properly. She loudly tells how her husband would come home in the dead of night, strike a match and pull back the sheets to see her lying there in the nude.

"Well, one day I put this raccoon skin down there see...." I am at a loss to shut her up. The whole ward of women is tittering at her humor and my embarrassment. I beat a hasty retreat.

"That was wonderful," I hear her telling the laughing ward, "he examined everything, just everything." I learn later the woman has

Korsakoff's Confabulatory Syndrome where humor of this sort masks memory impairment, and where there is sexual disinhibition! I am however too red faced to return to that particular ward too soon. The nurses are very amused too.

22

The Tea Party

A fine rheumatologist is precepting our group of eight students.

He has even invited us to his home. He talks about the Royal College specialty board examinations and their high failure rate. He will never participate in those, he says, for he cannot pass such judgment on the careers of young doctors. The Boards are something far off, but to be greatly feared. Heavens, I don't even have my MD yet a year and a half away and we have to start sweating for Boards.

Dr. O'Gryzlo is a fine physician however, and he is the only one to honor us with a tutorial at his home. I admire him, his clinical precision and his professional teaching skills. I would like to be like him.

Our group arrives at Dr. O'Gryzlo's home in East Toronto. It is Friday evening. We are greeted by his wife and we are seated in a comfortable living room. We are to be served tea. Dr. O'Gryzlo comes in and sits down. After chatting with us for a few minutes, he calls to his daughters who are also home. My mouth drops as two exquisitely lovely girls come into the room. The eldest is perfect for me. The right size, the right laugh, color, skin, figure. Oh God! I am in love. The professor's daughter and I love her. Dr. O'Gryzlo's tutorial is lost to me as his daughter wafts back and forth about the room hostessing and listening.

As Dr. O'Gryzlo, the revered professor, leaves the room to get some notes, I find his daughters and wife consider him an absent minded professor, in need of someone to keep his coat buttoned.

The situation is quite amusing. We, students, hold the professor in such esteem and his family considers him as bumbling as my own father.

I leave the tutorial, grateful for this attention by a man who epitomizes medicine to me and I am almost in a swoon over his daughter.

For days, I have my hand near the phone. I must call her. I must! But I am too intimidated. She is the professor's daughter. She is sophisticated, not Jewish, upper class. I am a poor medical student with one eye, no car, no money, no time.

God help me, I pass her up. Damn! Dr. O'Gryzlo wouldn't have minded. He probably wanted to set his girls up with a future doctor. I am overwhelmed. Like Linda all over again. I can't grow up!

23

Beating The Systems

This year has gone by with such rapidity that I cannot remember where it begins and ends. I have an oral in Medicine coming up and am nervous about this. It will mainly stress physical examination. We have conducted so many of these that it should not be terribly difficult. We have painstakingly covered each system over and over again. The cardiovascular system, nervous system, pulmonary system, digestive system, hemopoietic system, ear, nose and throat, reproductive system, covering just about all contingencies. On the day of the exam, I find there is still another system that someone was examined on a year or two years ago. No one has taught us about this one and it is not listed in our little green physical exam pamphlet. It is the locomotor system. What a poor sap that got hit with that one, I muse.

Anxiously, we wait in the ward corridor for our patient assignments for this final of third Meds. At last, it is my turn and a resident in medicine introduces himself and with a clipboard leads me to a female patient pleasantly sitting up in her bed. She is rather obese and seems a little nervous as I gingerly approach.

"Okay," says the medical resident, "you can work up Mrs. Green here. I'm sure she will be helpful to you. Examine her locomotor system and your examiners will be along in about ten minutes."

I am dumbstruck. The resident could have fired a gun at me.

I am the poor sap they will be talking about years from now. What is a "locomotor system?" Gradually, I recover from stupor and begin to ask questions about movement.

"I have rheumatoid arthritis," says Mrs. Green, "and I have a heart murmur associated with it."

This is some relief to me, although I am not being examined today for diagnostic skill. I can concentrate on a disorder of the joints and can coherently discuss a related problem of the condition. Actually, I do not fare too badly on the oral as it turns out with Mrs. Green's help, and I buy her a small plant the next day.

In Pediatrics, I make a diagnosis of fibrocystic disease in a small child and actually get an A for my final mark.

For a while, I think again of becoming a pediatrician, which I had early on decided to do but which I had tabled after seeing a number of deformed child monsters earlier in the year on a tour of a special pediatric floor.

And so another year has flitted by.

24

Practice Makes Perfect

or, A Kick In Time

Another summer has come and gone and I am back at school. Fourth Meds.

I have had my other operation and no longer need contact lenses. I now have both my eyes. I have another graft and this time it is positioned as a square, unlike the diamond arrangement in my right eye. My vision is somewhat better in my left than my right eye. Perhaps that is due to the eyes that Mr. Antonio had brought with him from the Syracuse eye bank. I had waited ten days for an eye and as I began to fear I could not be ready for school on time, I received word that Dr. Castroviejo had an eye for me. Mr. Antonio had arrived. He required a corneal graft like me and brought the two fresh eyes in an ice bucket (in ice) from Syracuse where they had just been extracted from a seventeen year old boy killed in a car crash. How strange to know of one's donor. How strange to have waited for this youth to die. He was alive and vital when I had commenced my ten day wait, my ten day inconvenience. He had died to end my inconvenience. Mr. Antonio was operated on at 8 a.m. the next day, I at 5 p.m.

And here I am back in class, fresh from surgery, like nothing had happened. I wear glasses and some people don't seem to recognize me. Other than that, the speed of events moves me along. The operations are history.

Dr. Castroviejo did let me watch him perform surgery. It was indeed a performance in his operating room surrounded by an observation platform equipped with binoculars. I, however, as a "doctor" was permitted to scrub up and look over his shoulder.

The performance was first class, watching, with my new eyes, someone else on the table. The incredible stitching of the famous and skilled surgeon was a thrill for a young medical student to watch. But to be a great doctor like this man seemed and seems so far off. I am a mere student, can I ever be any sort of a doctor?

With my eyesight returned, I lapse into a passivity in my final year of school. Rather than a final surge, I find I have little energy to apply myself in this last phase. Things are easier for me and my interest in medical matters is diverted to other things and now I coast along. It is not only I who do this. Many of the students do, for the final year is to a large extent anti-climactic. Passing this year, on the one hand, is almost a certainty after three rough years, though the idea of shifting from student to doctor in eight months is an impossible thing to comprehend.

I need a vacation so badly, but that is impossible and things move on inexorably. How strange now the end is in sight. It feels so unreal.

The final year is heavily clinical and practical. I do not have much of a taste for blood and am not very thrilled with running gastric tubes down my colleagues' noses. Freddy Hasimi, a small skinny Persian volunteer, has a tube run down his stomach through his nose and (Ha! Ha!) it comes out his mouth and it is dangling there with him gagging. It is quite funny.

I am relieved that by some peculiarity, our group has missed a tour of blood drawing and helping to set up IVs. I have no wish to stick people. Unfortunately, this 4th Meds "lucky break" will cost me dearly in the first few months of internship where bloodletting and IVs comprise much of the duty of an intern. I do not think of this now. I take two or three unsuccessful stabs at Ken's forearm for blood and do not get any. That is my total experience in getting blood. I am not used to my glasses and though I am considered to have a "beautiful" operative result, I still have some astigmatism and therefore could not be a surgeon, even though three months of surgery would be a part of internship. My astigmatism also makes hitting veins problematic.

Some of us have assisted in surgical procedures by now. I have watched a number of operations, but have not really done anything except scrub up and peer over someone's shoulder. No one has fainted in surgery. Actually, it is boring.

Much more fascinating I find is OB-GYN. That is rather fun, though we are all nervous. I get to hold a newborn baby or two. The birth process as theoretically described becomes alive and this is indeed an experience. We are often yelled at by bad tempered OB residents who have had no sleep or we are shunned by charge nurses. A child is born in bed, a precipitant birth. We joke loudly about this. A nurse angrily shushes us. It is not good to broadcast this. The hospital will not look good.

Most births we see proceed normally. The fetus twists and turns as it says in the books, angling its way out of the birth passage. Occasionally, it shoots out and virtually has to be caught, in a precipitant labor. This only occurs after more than one child, never in a first birth.

Some of the recent immigrant women when pregnant do not come into the hospital till they are at the point of delivery. Often these women shoot the babies out and there is no time for drapes or prep. This is accompanied with a full bowel movement and is a very unpleasant and primitive delivery. There are quite a few of these in fourth Meds.

Dr. Smith is an excellent orthopedic surgeon and an interesting teacher. He is also arrogant and very rich. He drives a huge Cadillac and flashes his affluence. I am impressed with his skill, though do not like him as a person. He takes us to the private ward at Mount Sinai to see one of his patients. She is a stunning, dewy, young woman in a sheer nightgown (which nonetheless is not totally revealing). There is something moist and succulent about her. We are all immobilized by her beauty and gingerly move her ankle under Smith's instructions. We do not do a good job. She is too beautiful. Beautiful women often do not get the best medical treatment because of the awe their looks inspire. We overreact, stopping ourselves from being too thorough because we are afraid of our impulses; therefore we are not thorough enough. I am sure no one has given this woman a routine rectal for instance ("no examination is complete without an examination of all the orifices").

The pranksterism continues. Larry sees a fellow student bending over in a white lab coat and kicks him in the ass. It is a professor, a case of mistaken identity. A late faux pas. It is the Chief of Surgery for God's sake! How embarrassing! Oh, what explanations!

"Doctor, what kind of behavior is this?"

"Oh, geez, Sir, I really am sorry.....I thought..." And so it goes.

Some maturity has occurred. No one, for instance, has for some time fed Nadine (an Hungarian immigrant) a prurient English phrase to be innocently inserted into an otherwise intelligent question. She was always so good for that. The best straight man you could ever find. Now it wouldn't be quite so funny since she is almost a doctor.

The Precision of Science

In this final year, Pathological Chemistry is the primary academic course and is a worry. This course requires a certain degree of thought and intelligence, which need not be employed to a great extent in other areas.

Chemistry is altogether the most scientific of the courses in medical school although there is a good deal of rote memory also required to learn the "language of chemistry" so to speak.

Chemistry in Premeds was taught by Professor Lister, an Englishman, who was something of a genius. (It did not help us that his name was the same as the eminent discoverer of asepsis).

That was called Physical Chemistry. We were allowed to use our texts and notes on exams and still found the course a struggle, though more stimulating than most.

Roy, in the course of an experiment, brewed a beaker of tea and called over an instructor.

"Hey," he shouts, "this stuff's gone brown."

Suddenly, he grabs the beaker off the flame and downs it with a gulp. The instructor (known as "Sweater," since he always wore a sweater) gasps and blanches, thinking Roy is committing suicide by ingesting a toxic chemical. He is laughingly reassured before he himself explodes.

Brian McGrath's famous experiment with sodium pellets and water was another chemical landmark in Premeds. In the course of a complex experiment, Brian takes a break from the assigned activity. He sets up a large beaker of water and gingerly drops sodium pellets into the beaker. They spin crazily and give off sparks and his bench mates are amused. "What a card!" As he is thus conducting his own experiment and deeply engrossed in this, along comes Professor Lister who softly walks up behind him and looks over his shoulder. The class is silent with this plot, and Brian continues to drop in pellets, which crackle, hum and spin. Finally, he looks up to find the professor peering down at him.

"Uh, hello, Sir," he says.

The class bursts out laughing as Lister good naturedly advises Brian to get on with the assigned task if he wishes ever to escape Premeds.

At times, I feel I am back in high school, back in Sleepy's class, copying down his formulae for passing the grade thirteen exam. He was a cynical former Royal Air Force pilot who ought to have been W.C. Fields' partner, red nose and all. Empty gin bottles were at times seen in his waste basket. We were all such silly school children to him. His perfunctory teaching did get me through the exams but certainly without any pleasure of discovery.

On one of his tests, I do two exams instead of one, finding the going inordinately tough. Later, I find I missed his preamble. There were two different exams to prevent bench mates from copying one another since Sleepy certainly did not believe in the honor system for his motley group of students. In Premeds, there was Physical Chem and Organic Chem. In Meds, we have had Biochemistry at some length, and now we have Pathological Chemistry, which is not unrelated. We learn or attempt to learn Liver Chemistry, Kidney Chemistry, acid base balance (metabolism) and go into various disease entities such as diabetes, cirrhosis and nephritis. The course is not too difficult except for the final practical examination, which was another situation inspiring inordinate anticipatory dread.

I find in the actual proceedings I can contend with most of what is thrown at me. However, the last part of the exam, worth fifty percent of the marks, requires performance of an on-site experiment and one must obtain a lab value using a colorimetric reading.

That is, the experimental substance, (in this case blood) when mixed in a particular way would form a particular color, a light brown. The colorimeter would measure the density of this solution and give a reading from 0 to 50, let us say.

I diligently perform my experiment under the stress of the practical exam. Oddly however, my end solution is very dark brown and, God help me, everyone else's seems to be light pinkish brown. I go to the colorimeter and read 10.6. I know this cannot be and therefore, despairing I put down 7.23, estimating from the array of test tubes of my colleagues, but an absolutely blind guess. I am crushed, for I feel I may not even be able to pass the exam. Perhaps I will just pass. I leave. I do not want to hear the right answer.

The exam marks are posted one week later. I am in despair. There have been many failures. Someone is smiling at me. "Are you making a comeback?" Again, I have got the highest mark in class, the second of two times. The correct reading, which I guessed at, was 7.23! Only I got it exactly. Only I got one hundred on the lab practical exam!

26

The End is Near

"6T3?" Auntie Renee laughed when I wore that jacket in the drugstore in 1957. It was a black corduroy jacket with bright red lettering, 6T3 on one sleeve, U of T on the other and MEDICINE across the back. When Jerry Cooper and another Meds student wore their 6T2 jackets driving across country one summer, they were stopped in Saskatchewan by local police.

"Okay, you boys. We know the gang from Medicine Hat is in the area. We don't want trouble now."

The two youths had considerable difficulty proving they were in Medicine and not the Medicine Hat gang.

The jacket for awhile was a part of my identity. I am a Meds student, I said. It proclaimed this garishly, but by God, I earned it! I kept it for years till someone named Ann tore it in half but that's another story.

Now it was, unbelievably, 1963 and final exams were near.

These would be combined licensure as well as final university examinations.

I am at another autopsy. These things have become routine. I have little trepidation here and have to get a card signed signifying I have attended two of these to complete a requirement of the Meds school. This autopsy is just damn hard work at which I assist, pulling up ribs and pulling out viscera. I have to leave the room when the skull is opened though, for close up, the smell is beyond belief and I start gagging. It is the smell though not the situation that causes this and even now as I write and recollect, I can still remember the smell and I feel slightly nauseous.

Back at the school. There is a group of classmates talking with worried looks on their faces. What is up? Something has happened. I cannot fathom what it is. No one volunteers information.

"Hey, what's happened?" I ask. "Charlie Short has killed himself."

He did not make it. Dr. Duckworth's prediction is one hundred percent.

Three weeks before our final licensure exams, we have a suicide.

Charlie was an affable man though quiet and a good student. No one seemed to know him well but I had talked with him a fair bit and had no inkling he would do this. We were virtually doctors and he waited right to the end. His wife was three months pregnant also.

"What did he do?"

I need to know this. He was in the bathtub. He dissected out his femoral artery (in the groin) and severed it. That's as good as the girl who sliced her carotid. Charlie was just as good an anatomy student. Dr. Duckworth was such a good teacher. I think his students were really inspired.

27

Light at the End of the Tunnel

The final exams are anticlimactic. They are hard work, but there would be no failures after this investment. One might have to take a supplemental exam at worst, but an MD was now assured. All the same, I am exhausted and drained and can barely perform.

My perverse fate has me faced with impossibilities on some of the orals. No one would ask for a classification of ovarian tumors, I had been assured. Oh well, they asked me. I get a C in OB-GYN, the subject I probably liked best. I do not like Psychiatry, so poorly taught at school. Nevertheless, hoping it is a lot better elsewhere, I have more or less decided to pursue this as a career.

My final marks are not outstanding. Again I get a consistent B average but have done less well finally with both my eyes than I had done severely handicapped. I had had an easier year and had made little study effort since previous years had been a grim effort. I coasted.

I do well in Internal Medicine since I diagnose (by luck) a mycotic aneurysm of the groin. I did not even know what that was but I said when pressed,

"That's an aneurysm." "What kind?"

"Mycotic," I answer devoid of any other thought.

That is the correct answer. I am not able to answer further questions about mycotic aneurysms very well, so do not do outstandingly well, but the examiners are impressed with my diagnostic deductive ability and tell me so. I am pleased. Ken had asked me a few hours earlier if I knew anything about mycotic aneurysms. I didn't.

"What is it?" I had asked.

He told me but l hadn't paid attention. (It is an arterial weakening caused by a bacterial embolus thrown off a diseased heart valve.)

But when the examiners asked what kind of aneurysm, l had answered "mycotic" since that was in my mind. Thank you Ken.

In Pedes, I, oddly, get another Fibrocystic disease. An infant this time however. These children have a genetic lung disease with salt loss as concomitant. I tell the examiner I licked the child and tasted salt. He thinks this is very funny and shouts it over to another examiner. I am beyond embarrassment.

But I do well on the clinical part.

Pediatric Radiology is another matter and I net a B grade overall.

The exams are over. I have passed. I have no supps. I am a doctor. I am a doctor!

On Thursday, we graduate and in one month, I begin a rotating internship at New Mount Sinai Hospital.

I have made it. Byron is now a lawyer. Charlie is dead.

Others have fallen away, through illness, marriage, distaste, breakdown. But I am an MD It is over!

I also have eyes. I can see!

PART II

THE INTERLUDE

or THEY PLAYED MUSIC BEFORE PEARL HARBOR

1

Interlude
On the Road

Two new doctors are heading west from Detroit into the sunset.

Medical school is behind us and we are in a shiny new 1963 Cadillac from a Detroit drive-away on a two week cross country trip. Larry, who is to be my roommate at Mount Sinai and who went through Vaughan Collegiate with me, is driving the new luxury car and has been doing so for the last thousand miles. We are in the land where charming JFK (a Hollywood star) is President; Stevenson did not make it.

"Come on, Dr. Tozman." Larry is coaxing me. "The thing practically drives itself."

I am very doubtful, for I have not driven for years and never with my new eyes.

"Larry," I argue, "you will be sorry. I haven't driven for a long time and I don't know if I can, just like that. Besides I have never even ridden in a car like this before, let alone driven one. All I've ever driven is a gearshift jalopy."

Larry is hard to convince for he is understandably tired. "All you have to do is steer, kiddo."

Finally, because I feel guilty at all the driving he has done while I have been merely an observer, I reluctantly agree and we shift positions.

Somehow at that moment, the car is like the internship looming imminently ahead. I long ago learned to drive and therefore know basically how one must operate a car of this sort. It is simply a matter of diving in and actually doing it.

Theoretically, I am also now a doctor having learned the basics, and all I must now do is jump right in.

The engine is on and the car is purring gently. I see the gear is on "P." I guess I have to move it to "D." I don't know what the "l," "2," and "N" are for, and Larry starts to explain, but then says they don't matter, and to just drive.

With my foot on the brake, I shift to "D" and then press the accelerator. We lurch forward and I am in a cold sweat. I am flashing hack to long ago with Frank and I had much more nerve then—the folly of youth. But we are on the road and the luxurious car is running smoother and steering easily. Larry is beginning to lean back and relax. The scenery is pretty as the gently curving road cuts through a rocky hill somewhere west of Chicago and I make a neat tight run along the curve, hugging the right lane. As we come out of the turn, there is, rather suddenly, an intersection. It is a wide one with cars waiting at right angles, and diagonally also, since three roads seem to meet here. My light is green, and I am proceeding through at about 30 mph.

Suddenly, all these cars confuse me. I see red lights on my right and left and diagonally and I am not certain it is I who have the right of way. I have not had highway experience since childhood and Larry seems to have thought I need no coaching.

Abruptly, in a panic, I throw the brake and since they are power brakes with instant response, which I have heretofore never employed, the car screeches to a dead halt and in slow motion, I discern Larry's contorted face flat up against the windshield.

Then his body falls back and he is sitting in his seat with a very surprised countenance. He is unhurt or not very hurt having received a slap comparable to what more than one Toronto Jewish girl had by now delivered to his countenance with equivalent intensity; however, he certainly does not seem pleased. He says nothing though and after some interminable seconds lapse, he opens his door gets out and comes around to my side.

"Move over," he says. And we are once again on our way. I do not get to drive for the rest of the trip. I sure hope I do better with the internship.

2

Bright Lights, Tight Tights

We are in Las Vegas now. Our cross country trip has been exceedingly fast. We are having a burger at a table outside beside our fancy Cadillac. Everything here seems to have a slot-machine motif, parking meters, cash registers, postal boxes. While I am munching my hamburger, I note that Larry has started talking to a woman. Rather she has started talking to him, for she apparently was eyeing us as we drove our luxurious vehicle into the parking space. She is a very pretty woman, tall and slim and, so we discover, she is a Las Vegas showgirl. It is evident that she thinks we are loaded, not having noticed the "DEALER" sign on our caddy license plates. She seems to be offering to accompany us to Los Angeles and to be proffering herself to do naughty things. I am suspicious that there may be something to pay at the end of it. Larry, however, is ready to accede to her importuning until she mentions her "boyfriend" who is apparently a local Mafia hit man from whom she wishes to abscond. Even Larry now begins to cool to the idea of having her along. She would get wise to our lack of money fast enough and why have a scene that could end in death? We beat a hasty retreat making whatever lame excuses suited the moment.

I find "Vegas" with no money is no more exciting than any other carnival and am sorry we did not opt for the Grand Canyon instead (our mileage allowance would not permit both). Larry however seems excited by the place with its gaudy lights and slot machines. He starts putting quarters into a machine and I start to get worried. His eyes are very red. I know he is tired, but now they look glazed too. Geez, he is really going crazy. I yank him away and we watch a strip show in a bar—a poor man's Las Vegas show. It is not bad, but small fixings compared to the headline acts. Larry is heading back to the slot machines and I practically have to wrestle with him to wrench him away. Maybe he hurt his head on the windshield after all.

Finally, thankfully, we are back on the road and soon we will be in LA.

3

Welcome to LA. We Stop for a Sandwich

Two and one half days and nights have passed since we left Toronto, and we have entered Los Angeles. We have spent hours crossing the dusty desert on the last leg of our trip. Our mileage is just under the allowance though we do not have to deliver the car for several days since we crossed so rapidly. We are tired and dirty for we had slept for two nights in the car.

Larry has arranged with some former St. Michael's nurses to be put up at their place and I will stay for a few days in a cheap hotel near my sister's place. Hollywood & Vine are as unimpressive as ever, just two ordinary streets crossing. How disappointing is reality compared to the mystique.

I do not know where Larry is going to sleep since there are six nurses living in a two bedroom apartment. Oh well, I am sure he will manage. These Toronto girls seem pretty wild out here in California. They had a curfew at St. Michael's Catholic Nursing School and they are really letting loose here. They have a clothesline set up across one end of the living room with four bottles hanging from it filled with gin. They saw that in a movie and reality and fiction blend here. Larry imbibes some, but I do not. It's the wrong time of day I guess. The girls allege that they are on constant vacation here and act it. They have a swimming pool and are running back and forth in skimpy bathing suits.

Doreen, one of the nurses, has a boyfriend whom we meet. He is an affable Jewish guy who is an American history major at UCLA though rather older than the usual Canadian undergraduate since he has been in the army. In keeping with the bizarreness of Hollywood, this fellow, Bernard, works in a crematorium part time preparing what he calls "Sandwich Specials," namely a corpse (loved one) between two wood boards—a cheaper way to go.

Bernard and the girls are impressed with our car and so we are coaxed to drive to Tijuana in it. The mileage problem is easily rectified since Bernard was in the U.S. Army motor pool and he disconnects the odometer. Thus Bernard, Doreen, Larry, another nurse Stephanie, plus my sister, Gilda, now on the scene, and I all head for Mexico in a Cadillac that no longer registers miles travelled.

4

Tijuana

Tijuana, which I am told does not represent Mexico, is a seedy border town. I am appalled by the poverty and indignity that the "Yankees" just to the north have not only permitted but have had a hand in. The place abounds with beggars and whoremongers and ailing people, so it seems. American military personnel are present too in as great numbers as the natives.

Old American cars and buses clank and chug through the dusty streets. Most of the cars are taxis. The buses are loaded with disheveled looking locals.

We see a bar, which advertises, we gather, an erotic cabaret and we all go inside. It is simply a dingy strip joint, we find, and moreover, except for a solitary man at a table with a flower in a glass jar, we comprise the entire audience. We are seated on the runway.

We wait for a hot south-of-the-border strip. All I have ever seen were pasties and G-String numbers and this town is supposed to be wide open. Perhaps something lascivious will materialize. We wait in the dimly lit room sipping weak beer but no strippers appear. There is some activity, but still no torrid show. Wow there is shouting—an argument. A shrill voice is shouting in Spanish.

"What is it Bernard?" Bernard speaks some Spanish. Our stripper, it seems, refuses to perform tonight. There is one stripper and she is refusing to come out. More shouting. At last, however, Conchita accedes and makes a haughty entrance.

Conchita is an attractive, brown skinned woman who walks onto the runway in panties and bra. There are no preliminaries. She promptly removes her bra and walks about topless, displaying unpastied brown nipples. Somehow the scene is comparable to surreptitiously looking into a tenement window on a hot night at a woman across the way going about her business. There is very little eroticism here and one half expects Conchita to set up an ironing board. However, now on stage, Conchita has decided after all to give us our money's worth, which she does by lowering her white plain panties below her pubic region and crouching obscenely. Next, she begins picking at her pubic hairs and throwing them into the air.

Doreen has by now lifted her sweater over her head to cover her face. The girls are practically in a faint with embarrassment. "Oh, my God," squeals Stephanie, "a hair has fallen in my drink." Conchita is amused by our reaction and is laughing and calling in Spanish. She is suggesting Stephanie give her drink to the lone male who would be pleased to consume it. We move on rather quickly.

In the street once more, we learn there is a bullfight at the Coliseum. None of us have seen such a spectacle and so we decide to try and get tickets. We hail a beat up taxi and pay one dollar per person as demanded. Shortly thereafter, we are deposited at a round bullring coliseum affair—a considerably scaled down version of the one Tyrone Power/Ava Gardner pranced around in "The Brave Bulls." Here we are, informed first that we are too late. Next, we are told we can get in if we pay four dollars per person. As we begin to walk away, the ticket man calls up and we promptly find ourselves in the coliseum for fifty cents each. It dawns on us that one is not expected to pay the stated price for anything.

The spectacle is in any case almost over. Only one bull is left. As the poor beast enters the ring, I find all my sympathies are with it. It is an old bull who nonetheless is a proud animal. I am filled with revulsion at the ecstatic and hysterical clamoring of the crowd, tourists and natives, lusting for blood.

The black animal stands there snorting. It is a raggy but haughty beast. I wince as the picadors throw their little spears into him and he starts in pain and anger but he seems confused and does not attack the matador. The matador poises his sword to run the poor bull, placidly snorting, through the back of the neck as he lowers his head. The matador strikes. Oh God, he botches it! The crowd oohs. The sword has hit the bull's head striking bone and glancing off. The sword has fallen on the ground. The bull backs away, hurt and confused. This is butchery. Another thrust through the neck and the poor animal staggers and falls. It is still by no means dead and the red blood darkly trickles down the black hide. A third sword thrust finishes off the beast and there is massive cheering and throwing of hats and pillows in the air. The ears and tail are cut off by the other butchers and presented to the noble matador. Why are they cheering this? I am sick and disgusted.

I am happy to be out of the ugly coliseum and in a cab heading away from the horrible scene. Initiated now to bartering, we have paid this cab driver one dollar to transport the six of us, rather than the dollar each we paid on arrival. He is quite satisfied with this for the short ride.

Back at the marketplace, we buy little souvenirs and some tequila at outrageously low prices. Gilda buys a silk scarf from a boy who asks eight dollars. "I'll give you fifty cents," she responded. He is insulted but lets her have it finally for two dollars. It is worth at least fifteen.

It is twilight and we are getting ready to head back. The three girls have accompanied us for the last several hours and we wish to look around a little by ourselves. We see the women are occupied in a shoe store and tell them we are going for a quick walk. They are busy trying on shoes and therefore do not protest, in fact, hardly notice. As the three of us start along the main street, we are accosted literally by a score of body hawkers, men and women alike. I have never seen anything like this. Prostitution is the main business of this town.

"Hey, you want my young seester?"

We go into a bar and three women jump on us at a signal from the manager. Bernard and Larry have two pretty girls on their knee and are getting free feels. One can thoroughly examine the merchandise here before putting money down. Larry is putting his fingers right in. I, however, get a toothless hag grabbing at me whom I have to fight off. Sex is sex they seem to think.

Do most men fuck anything that moves?

As we are returning to the shoe store, a very pretty young girl approaches us and offers herself for one dollar each. We converse with her but are not buying. One dollar each she begs. There are tears in her eyes. Larry, cruel bastard that he is, says, "How about one dollar for all three?" The girl agrees my God, sex is so cheap here! I guess life is too. At that price though we don't want it. We move off. I am sorry I did not give her something. If only I had some money. I should have given her a dollar anyway.

"Come on, come on; the girls are waiting."

They are waiting and hopping mad at our hour's stroll. "Where the hell were you?" fumes Gilda at me.

We return to the border and the girls plus Bernard re-enter the U.S. Larry and I surprisingly find we have explaining to do. Canadians at the Mexican border do not pass freely in and out, and Larry, who is queried first, is told to stand aside. I have visions of being stranded in an ugly foreign city and maybe murdered here. However, as I corroborate Larry's sheepish story to the immigration officer, he finally lets us through. We get into our Cadillac and return to LA. Bernard reconnects the odometer and next day we deliver the car.

5

In The Pink

We are heading north towards the scenic route to San Francisco. We have another drive-away car, a pink Ford Thunderbird convertible and we will deliver this to a private owner in San Francisco. As we drive through LA., teenyboppers pull alongside and hoot at us in our pink swinger's car. The car is getting a terrific reaction. I am not sure how to respond. There are little blonde girls, the ones who wear bright lipstick and skin tight latex slacks, which look sprayed on and they are waving at us. I begin to worry that our pink car is identifying us as homosexuals or something. Gilda's girlfriends (the starlets) seem to engage in homosexual spotting as a pastime. Perhaps all the girls here try that.

"There goes one," they would say. "He doesn't look like that to me." Guilty until proven innocent in LA.

I am therefore not sure whether to be pleased or embarrassed by the attention our car is receiving. I wave gaily back to the girls (or do I wave gayly). The girls giggle and rev their engine.

Up the coast, we pass through the beautiful Big Sur area. We are delayed by a flat tire and there is no spare! Our car is stalled on a precipitous curve. Fortunately, a service station nearby bails us out for five dollars and we continue through Big Sur and Monterey. The scenery is gorgeous with the Pacific Ocean to our left and below the precipice. The waves smash against the rocks and the spray shoots high into the air. It is by far the most beautiful terrain I have ever seen, more so I think than the mountains whose grandeur is static. We do not stop enroute other than to look at the scenery and I barely notice signs that say, "SUPPORT YOUR LOCAL POLICE," and "NO BEARDS OR LONG HAIR ALLOWED."

Up the coast, we pass by San Jose, and are soon in Palo Alto.

We look around here briefly, for I have thoughts of doing my residency at Stanford University. Palo Alto looks like a university town—I think like Ann Arbor. It is not however.

The university is on a quiet, country-like campus and the medical center is gracefully architectured in a Spanish motif.

Soon we are in San Francisco, which I find lovely and picturesque. The Golden Gate Bridge is a graceful span and we cross it to view the city from Sausalito. It is a fairyland in the twilight as little white houses on the hills light up. I do not notice sleazy Market Street, nor realize the beautiful bridge is probably the world's greatest suicide lure being the last jumping off point for scores of people.

The cable cars are pretty and quaint, a lovely tourist attraction, but they are something else when used as a primary vehicle to get to work in the morning. The cable man does bump me unpleasantly as he hauls the gear lever back in the middle of the aisle and no apologies, but I am enjoying myself.

6

Berkeley and The Nude Model

Dave is a former Vaughan Collegiate classmate taking his PhD in Math at Berkeley. He meets us in San Francisco in a broken down jalopy, one much closer to what I had cut my teeth on.

Dave, a mathematician, is something of an eccentric and a symbolic radical. That is, he looks radical, making conservatives angry at him, though he espouses no political ideology. He drives a wrecked car and has a rather unkempt beard. He lives in a type of commune in Berkeley immediately discernible from all the rest of the neat and well kept houses on the block by its overgrown, haunted appearance and freaky looking people, one of whom, a young woman, is sitting on the stoop as we pull up.

The girl named Angela is also unkempt and looks rather "witchy." She would have been in place as a member of the Manson clan of that era.

She greets us in a low keyed way. She is not unpretty—the opposite she is quite pretty and I find she had been considered a brilliant student till about a year ago when she dropped out. Now she does part-time work at the Berkeley School of Fine Arts as a nude model.

I talk with her in the kitchen surrounded by layers of inch thick dirt and residue and unwashed dishes and later in the garden of overgrown crab grass and weeds. At night we have a little party and Angela and I down a bottle of gin together and before long, I am drunk out of my mind, more than ever before in my life. So much so that we end up under a table engaging in indecorous behavior, too drunk to care who notices.

I awake in the morning in a bed, and cannot remember how I got here.

"Don't let this give you any ideas," says Angela.

This morning she is cold and distant. She is getting ready to go on her nude modeling job.

"Why do you have to do that?" I ask. She is intelligent and attractive and crazy.

She smiles at me. "Aren't you a silly boy."

Larry and I look at the bulletin board at Berkeley. The campus is swarming with people and there are various protest signs in abundance. There are no rides east. I am a little worried for I cannot afford fare back home. We check the local paper and fortunately find a ride. It is a middle-aged natty gentleman wanting to share driving back east. This is strangely easy and by God, he has a new Lincoln Continental, a silver one. Larry and he get on famously. They are much alike materialistic and talkative. Larry and the man share the driving and I spend most of the 2200 miles in the back seat.

At Toledo, we drop off and after noting the local color (militant blacks in flashy chrome trimmed cars with skull and cross bone aerial flags, plus whitewalls, mud guards and animal skins, eyeing us darkly and suspiciously), we hop a bus east and before long, we are back safe and sound in Toronto.

Psychiatrist, Surgeon, Blind-man, Seer, Life-Force, Death-Force ever near. Devil, Angel reach the Sky, Ever be afraid to Die.

Darkness, Daylight, Night's Travail, Will he live to tell the Tale?

Cancer eats your brain away, Shall he live another Day?

Closer, Reaper, Sword in hand Ever take I your command, Ever live, and ever die.

Cast a spell, and touch the Sky.

Flecks of blood adorn his coat Coughed up from a dead man's throat. Hide the Horror, wash the cloak!

Flush away the dead man's joke.

Weary traveler all in white, Can you last another night?

Somewhere, somehow flowers bloom But never here in pallid gloom. Stillborn, Newborn, Life's Rebirth, How little is a dead man worth?

PART III

HEALER SEER DOER
-PSYCHIATRIST, SURGEON, BLINDMAN, SEER

1

Dracula—
Is It All In Vein?

"Oh No, not you again." The poor, white-faced man lies there unhappily viewing me and my set of syringes and needles.

"Yes, I'm afraid so," I say wearily. "Come on, we have to do it."

The poor man turns his head away and submits and I fit the steel needle, 20 bore, into the glass syringe to draw his blood. I put on the tourniquet and wait for the vein to come up, then I swab the vein. Then I aim and nervously put the needle into the skin. "Shit," it doesn't penetrate the vein. Oh God, now there's a hematoma. I release the tourniquet. The man cries out in pain and looks very ill. Heaven help me, I am going to kill this man—he has had a heart attack. They have all had heart attacks on Medicine. They are all in their 50s, 60s, or 70s and they have all had heart attacks. The whole service is that. I try again. The same luck. I am desperate.

Mrs. McBride is standing by. She is a matronly head nurse and anxiously looks on. I am another new intern and a headache for her, I realize, wet behind the ears as I am. She is sympathetic, however, and does not seem judgmental. She doesn't ask me, "Didn't they teach you to take blood?"

"No, you see we missed our rotation in fourth Meds, the only place where it was taught...."

The medical residents have shown us, however, but it is, "show it, do it, teach it" and now two weeks later I am presumed good enough to teach it. And suddenly here I am in charge of IVs.

The nurses, many who are adept at this, are forbidden to do it and I am the bloodletter and intravenous setter upper and fixer, and heaven help me, I cannot get those needles in. For two weeks I have been sticking people and making hematomas. How have I (and they) survived the last two weeks?

Finally, McBride can stand it no longer. She takes syringe and needle from me and in a flash she has the vein and the dark venous blood is filling the syringe. I stand by relieved and helpless. I am a doctor.

I am a junior intern at Mount Sinai Hospital. All of my anatomy partners are here too, as is Larry. Two women have also elected Mount Sinai, Carole and Wilma. Carole is a beautiful, statuesque blonde. She is slim and curvy and competent and has no problem with the veins or anything else I can see. "When you have it, you have it." Wilma, is a clutsy little dame with a good heart and she does her IVs possibly worse than me. At times I see her lying transversely atop a patient trying to put a needle in the opposite forearm. Occasionally, I see a vertically placed needle, as though the patient had been shot by a dart and note it is her work. I am fond of her and I realize that she is handicapped by her abbreviated height (her "cross") as I am by my astigmatism.

I hear there are new needles—disposable ones—in some of the other hospitals and this would make life easier, but Mount Sinai has not yet received these. Consequently, we and the patients too must suffer with needles that are autoclaved and re-used and are therefore dull, grossly compounding our problem with IVs.

I am exhausted, enervated. Though it is a great relief to have incessant exams behind me, what I must now do is terrifying in quite another way. I have been on duty two different nights now and that is a ghastly experience. The residents have been more available than they will be in future so I have got through the two nights. Last night was one. Today I must work till five o'clock and then I can leave. I have had one hour's sleep in the last twenty-six and have six more hours on the day shift.

Around 1:00 p.m. I go to my room to lie down for a few minutes. I have had no lunch and do not want any. I have had a cup of coffee, half cream. I am thin and wan and fear I will waste away altogether. I lie on my bed in the pleasant residence connected to the hospital. Larry is my roommate and thank goodness he isn't here. There is no privacy—hardly ever.

I am away from the on-call lights, which I cannot avoid anywhere in the main hospital, and when this digital display flashes 359 I am beckoned to the phone, which has now become my enemy. Now I stare glumly at the black instrument, which has become a living thing in the last two weeks. Even as I stare, it rings and I am summoned to inject dye for an IVP. On I go—oh thank goodness this man's got good veins. I hit it first try and slowly inject the fluid.

I pass Carole in the hall. She is on surgery—the most taxing service and seems so cool. How pretty she is. She smiles at me and we commiserate. I would ask her to marry me but a psychiatrist caught her eye and did it already four years ago. She seems so composed and able, but even she looks tired today.

359, 359 is flashing. Please let it be five o'clock soon.

2

Mount Sinai is Co-ed

I have chosen Mount Sinai because it is small, clean and new. I had seriously considered St. Michael's for similar reasons and moreover I liked the nurses there and had dated many of them. I finally opted for Mount Sinai, the Jewish hospital, probably for the ethnic safety it represented as well. Next year I would leave Toronto, perhaps forever, and this may be the last time I can enjoy the protection of a small and culturally safe institution used by family and friends alike. It was here also that I was born, in the old building that is. I reason also that a smaller hospital will give us less work and more time off; however, I soon find that this assumption is flawed. We have a complement of twenty or so interns who cover everything and this means on every service we are on duty every other night and every other weekend, with the exception of present rotation, Medicine. On Medicine, I am on every third night. I find that the Toronto General residents are on every third night throughout because of their greater number. What work for two thousand dollars and room! And yet for the first time I am self-sufficient, with my loans deferred to the end of my training.

Mount Sinai has certain saving graces, however. Many attending physicians are very decent and the residents also. For good or ill, I also find I know many patients and from time to time a relative or a friend or a friend of a friend is attended by me. Since the institution has only just become a teaching hospital, the atmosphere is stimulating and enthusiastic.

The nurses at Mount Sinai are young and pretty, attracted by the new hospital, and that certainly is a real plus. There is also a nursing school, a two-year program with a residence attached to the hospital.

That is also not hard to take. The nurses are sweet and very friendly, most of them are just out of school. They wear neat, clean, starched white uniforms and the black headband identifies a qualified nurse as does a silver medallion. Some of the experienced nurses are ill-tempered. I quickly discover that whether I will sleep or not depends solely on the sensitivity of the duty nurse who will harass with useless calls and wake me if a bitch, or call only if a real emergency exists if a sweetheart, which lots fortunately are.

So far I have had no time to take advantage of this new world populated with its proper share of femininity. Emerging from the hermitage of medical school, not to mention my semi-blindness, I find the situation quite novel, and though taxed and exhausted I somehow feel a small flow of hope that perhaps the frustrations and futility in my life to now might metamorphose in some peculiar way. I am not sure what the future will bring, but I begin to feel, even though the cost might be high, the exciting throb of adventure. And this is something new.

3

Vogel and His Birds

My internship partner is someone different by chance—not Larry my anatomy and high school buddy. He is Lionel Vogel who, though Jewish and a graduate with us, is not a Toronto boy. He is from Kitchener, a town west of Toronto, which I had always believed was devoid of my ethnic counterparts. Lionel is a goodlooking young man with dark eyes and dark wavy hair and he boasts of an enviable reputation with women. In fact, if half his stories are true (and I think more than half are) he has screwed more women over the last year than I will do in a lifetime. All the nurses know him, smile at him, and wink at him.

He was a medical extern at a Catholic Hospital near his home town for the last two years and his escapades were legendary. While I was getting my eyes cut, he was screwing everything in sight. His credo was, "If it has a skirt, fuck it." Scottish highlanders be warned. "But" he confided to me, "I am not as bad as Tom (another classmate). His credo was, 'if it moves, fuck it!'"

Lionel's reputation was exceeded only by Willie Bakoo's, a Trinidadian medical student with us, now interning at Toronto Western. Bakoo, an affable black guy with a precise mind, was sexually outrageous and the envy of everyone.

"Why, I came three times last night with that white girl," he would tell me.

"Only three, Willie?"

"In one hour, what you want now?"

Willie told me he had a special scrapbook of his conquests.

It contained swatches of pubic hair. "Come on, Willie, you show that to me."

"Well, all right now. I'll show you—but don't you smell it—only I can do that".

I never get to see his scrapbook but he makes me laugh and I dearly envy his smooth way with women.

Lionel ran Willie a close second—no, come to think of it he probably was ahead of Willie. He was more psychopathic and there were all sorts of stories about him, some of them generated by him, other stories by the nurses.

He was quite amoral and knew it. He was not necessarily proud of this but was not bothered by it either. He had an exceedingly low opinion of women I think and despised them for giving in to his powerful seduction.

He tells me that the Mount Sinai nurses are whores and relates his adventures. He has hidden behind a curtain when the fiancé of one of the nurses barged in and he made it out the window.

A few years ago, working as an extern at the aformentioned Catholic hospital, he screwed a patient in her bed with curtains drawn and nuns wandering in the halls.

It wasn't even a private room.

"Well this dame just grabbed me and unzipped my fly. What could I do? And then she started licking it and sucking. Finally, I came. What a scene! So I said to her [hands on hips and looks stern], 'Now are you satisfied?'"

I was hoping that a fraction of Vogel's success with women might fall to me, but he is now engaged to be married to a Mount Sinai lab technician—a beautiful piece of course—and has toned down considerably.

This will last the year, long enough to preclude his being of use to me in that regard. My moral code is different than his anyway, but maybe I'm the sap.

4

A Firecracker

Gord and a friend, Peter, are visiting me in my on call apartment/room. Peter is being very jovial and friendly. I am irritated with him for drinking all my liquor and for being so deferential to me now. He's always been argumentative and challenging the entire time I have known him with the exception of the last month or so, since I have become a "real" doctor.

Shit, this piece of paper really seems to mean something to people. As Chamberlain said, "I have a piece of paper. ..." I am the same person, aren't I? Oh, his girlfriend, Marie, is here too. She asks me about her sore throat. I feel her glands (under her chin) and answer her questions matter-of-factly. She says in awe, "Now I realize you're a real doctor. Isn't that funny?"

"Sy," says Gord, "I want you to come to the Movement tonight. There's a new girl there for you. She's a friend of (red headed) Lillian's. It's too bad you weren't there last week though because Billy Putman has got her now. Anyway come on down and you'll see."

I am at once interested and suspicious. Gord has thrown a thing or two my way from time to time and he is my best friend, but he is also unreliable on occasion so I don't know. The "Movement" has become a pain in the neck and I am still persona non grata. But it might be worth dropping by in the eternal quest for a bit of ass. Especially since Mount Sinai has stimulated me but I have got nothing there so far.

We enter the bookstore and go into the back room—the cell.

Lillian's red hair is visible but it is difficult to take everything in, in the dim light.

Gord whispers to me, "the doll in the back—I was gonna fix you up with her."

I turn my head to look to the back row of folding chairs and see a blonde girl. She is sitting with Bill. Gee, that lets me out anyway doesn't it? At a quick glance while Ross Dawson is describing capitalist economy, I take in the blonde hair, backcombed up, the high forehead and white skin. She is a handsome woman. She is neatly and conservatively dressed. I could have given it a tumble, I muse.

Before long the meeting is over and Gord introduces me to the newcomer. "Ann Harvey, this is Dr. Tozman, Sy Tozman." A smile and a nod. I am glad I am presentable. We "doctors" had to wear shirts and ties all through medical school so it is a habit. The others are in jeans or casual clothes. I have on my old blue blazer with the school of medicine crest on it as well, which is an adaptation of English private school dress. This is fortuitous, I learn later, because Ann is English.

I do not talk to Ann that evening. We all go for coffee to a local cafe, and she sits opposite Bill. We volubly talk of pressing social issues and politics. We even talk of sex and religion. Harold Silver, the retarded man, garrulously interrupts and I worry lest we get kicked out of the cafe. I participate in animated discussions, but always in the corner of my eye, I see the little blonde, neat, well groomed and quiet, taking in the socialist radicals. She is a school teacher, Gord tells me later, and apparently she is going to leave the city in a month or two.

"Listen, Gord, why bother me about this dame? Billy's got her, hasn't he?"

"Yeah, it's too bad."

I eye his friend, Lillian. She is a pretty and stacked little redheaded Scottish girl. I wouldn't mind a piece of her for that matter.

Gord phones me later. "Look, Lillian says you should come to the big meeting next week at Kensington Hall. Can you make it?"

I am off duty next weekend so I can and decide to play along.

What can I lose, unless the RCMP raids us?

5

A Routine Physical

Others work from sun to sun, an intern's work is never done. My schedule is one night on, two off call duty. On call every third weekend—second call on Saturday, first call on Sunday or vice versa. There are six of us on this service—later there will be four and we will be on call every other night for the remaining nine months of internships.

Much of my work has to do with bloodletting—that is, drawing blood and setting up IVs. Also giving IV injections. Often I have to find a vein and it is a matter of life and death. Morphine and aminophylline are standard life-saving drugs for pulmonary edema in which a person literally drowns in his own fluid. These substances have to be put in fast and because the patient is in shock, the veins collapse, making things very difficult indeed at times.

Our major role as interns is to provide routine physical examinations for all patients, private or non-private, coming into the hospital. We also write admission orders, totally or in cooperation with the attending physicians. Since little more than one month has elapsed, I have had no deaths so far, but it could happen any day. Vogel had one a few days ago—a thirty-nine year old man whom he had admitted with a massive coronary. He seemed all right when I left the ward—I had talked to him and though he was in pain he seemed pretty good. But that night he went sour and Vogel and Dave Zippin, the first-year resident, worked on him and tried to save him but he died. All of us on Medicine were upset over losing this man who was so young. But I had been in that situation before in Med school and my involvement was peripheral.

359, 359. Dr. Jena calls me to tell me he is admitting a patient from the emergency. Dr. Jena is an Indian doctor and the chief medical resident. He is a serious and competent man and is helpful to us although his associate, also from India, Dr. Adana, is even more concerned for us.

Dr. Jena, I guess, is worn out and he is not as young as Adana or Zippin.

"Tozman," he says to me, "I am sending up a sixty-nine-year-old woman. She has had an M.I. [coronary] but she's stable now.

I've medicated her and I think she's OK. Examine her and give me a call back later."

I saunter up to the floor leisurely to do the routine physical, and enter the room where the patient has been brought. She is in the room by herself.

"Hello, I am...." Lord, she is purple. She is gurgling. Pulmonary edema!

God what do I do? Jena what have you done to me—where the fuck are you? "Get Jena" I shout to the nurse, Miss Scott.

Tourniquets quickly—one-quarter morphine. She is gurgling and foaming.

"Blood pressure is 60/50 and dropping doctor." "Trendelenburg—no we'll drown her—prop her up." Tourniquets on—IV tubing—siphon off some blood.

"She's drowning." "Find a vein—I got it, OK." Blood rushes in to the vacuum bottle. Jena arrives—"What happened Tozman??—OK, you're doing OK...."

But the patient isn't. She gasps and, Lord help me, she is dead! I am near tears and Jena too is crestfallen. After such activity, the three of us, the nurse and the two doctors, are quiet and the patient is still too. The purple color remains. The relatives are in the waiting room and I have the task of telling them. They didn't know of the drama that just transpired and they believe the patient will be all right.

"I am sorry," I say, "she is gone."

Shock. Hysteria. "NO, NO, NO." Tears and wailing.

The son is crushed and sobbing unremittingly. Helpless and shaken I back away and as soon as I can, I get off the ward.

Oh God, won't someone stroke me or comfort me?

6

If you Ann, Does That Mean Me Tarzan

I am not quite sure how this has transpired. We are in the intern's lounge at Mount Sinai—myself, Gord and Peter—and three girls, Doreen, Lillian and the new girl, Ann. The meeting at Kensington Hall is over and the speaker, a black militant from Detroit, has gone off with Ross Dawson and has by now been arrested by the RCMP for all I know. Ann started the evening with Bill, to whom I assumed she belonged, but now she seems to have ditched him—rather callously, I think—and has come with me. I am quite flattered, actually, but I wonder at this frivolous treatment of the poor guy, when they were practically married in my mind.

Other interns and residents are dropping in on our little party and are talking to our girls. I am pleased with this too since they all have their tongues hanging out of their mouths like a bunch of hungry dogs and it occurs to me that these girls are quite handsome. Lillian looks good with her neat little boobs and unbuttoned blouse down, which I peer surreptitiously from time to time. One of the interns whom I don't particularly like assumes the girls are not assigned to anyone in particular. I hear him say,

"Hey, I wouldn't mind a piece of that little blonde...."

I eye the little blonde, Ann. She is talking quietly to Gord in her soft voice with just a touch of an English accent. She is about five feet four, an inch or two taller than Lillian and that is a better height for me. Also it gives her nice proportions. She is neatly and conservatively dressed and seems to have a dewy quality, which a few very feminine women possess.

Ann and I do not talk a great deal for there are too many people and the atmosphere is too jolly. But now I have her phone number and I have told her I will call soon. She seems very receptive in her modest way and I am suspicious. Poor Bill.

The weekend is almost over and I will be back on duty. My father is a patient at Toronto Western Hospital, having had a cataract operation. His oculist is affiliated with Toronto Western so he is in a different hospital, not Mount Sinai.

My uncle Abie (uncle-in-law through my father's sister Fanny) is also in hospital—he has had a severe depression and they gave him ECT at the provincial mental hospital, that is "999" the famous address of the "crazy house" nearby.

Toronto Western is walking distance from Sinai, and the day is pleasant so I saunter over. I walk up the curved roadway to the Emergency entrance and enter the Emergency area. I am a doctor, and also I trained here as a student so I can use forbidden access ways. The ER is more active than Sinai's since it is a larger receiving hospital, the second largest in the city in fact. I see a trauma case on a stretcher moving to X-ray.

Pretty bloody—a car accident, I wince. God I hope I don't get that stuff when I am on ER. As I exit the passageway I see a colleague behind a desk. He is the intern on Emergency and my classmate. Shit, our class was so large, one hundred and fifty students—what's his name? I cannot think of his name—how embarrassing. Well, perhaps he won't see me. Ugh, no such luck. He is looking up. He has seen me. Now if I say nothing he will think I am snubbing him. Well, he doesn't have to know I don't know his name. I walk over to the plexiglass partition.

"Hi there," I say. "How's it going?"

He gets up and answers. "May I help you, sir?"

7

Let's Try Type O

I am on duty with David Zippin. He is taking me around on his procedures. We have done a spinal and got the cerebrospinal fluid cleanly for a change, not a bloody tap. I accompany David as he does a lung fluid aspiration with a long needle. There is still too much sticking people on Medicine otherwise I might consider Internal Medicine as my specialty.

I guess it will be Psychiatry. Soon I will have to write letters to Stanford, McGill, Bellevue, and so on. Psychiatry does not seem to exist in Toronto and our lectures on "molecules" as the basis for human behavior have left me very little the wiser. There is no Psychiatry rotation at all in this internship year.

David has gone off to the doctor's lounge. I am glad he is on with me because I know him well from school and his family knows mine so we are practically relatives. He is easy going, and I have no worries about calling him when necessary.

I am lying on the bed in my room across from the hospital. It is twilight and I am dozing. I have made rounds on the ward and all is quiet. I fall into a fitful slumber accompanied by dreams of Marty, of Linda, of Ann… and then I see flashes of red and eyes and blood is dripping on me, and suddenly I see them shooting a barrage of bullets or arrows—no, of needles, tiny needles in my face and penetrating my brain—my brain is on fire—a beat—a ringing, ringing. I awake with a gasp.

It is pitch black. It is the phone. That ugly, black, living phone. I reach for it and it falls off the table.

"Hello, Hello, Tozman, Tozman." A man's voice. Zippin.

"Oh, Zippin." I collect my thoughts; I put my voice in higher register to act awake.

"Yes, yes, you want me on the floor—I'll be right over." Groggily I get up and put my pants on. I take the outside route to the hospital since the summer weather is pleasant and the night air wakes me. It is 3:30 a.m.

On the ward I find David working on a patient and I help him. It is a woman. She is bleeding internally from ruptured esophageal veins in her throat. She is an alcoholic, I guess in her 50s and this condition is secondary to liver cirrhosis. Her skin is sallow from blood loss and I set up an IV, first taking blood for cross-match. She is shocky and I am glad to get a vein. I put in an 18 needle and we set up plasma. David is getting ready to pass a Blakemore. But her pressure is dropping fast—70/60, 60/50, 50/— "keep her legs up—tilt the bed more." "Pump that plasma."

"David she needs blood. What about type O? We'll never get the cross-match in time."

"No, no type O—we can't risk it. She'll coagulate and die." "David," I say in a low voice trying not to let the patient hear, "she'll die anyway."

I fiercely pump the plasma—she is splitting blood. "Oh, save me, save me, save me...," she pleads desperately. Her voice sounds far away. I'm trying—God help me. I'm trying.

We are working feverishly but with a last "save me" there is a gurgle and she is dead. "She's dead!" She asked me to save her and she's dead—she died right under my hand. Oh, how awful!

My white uniform is spattered with flecks of blood. I am worn and beaten. The nurses clean and prep the body. There are no relatives.

David leaves the floor and I fill out the death certificate and sign it. My second one.

As I walk off the floor, I see three pints of crossmatched blood coming up. "Oh well, better late than never," an aide glibly chirps.

"Is that right?" I reply.

8

To the Victor, the Spoils

I am at my parents' place. I will stay here the night and go back to the hospital in the morning. I am off tomorrow night too and then on duty Friday. I am sitting by the telephone making ready to call a girl. How many times have I done this, speaking to women I do not know at all or barely know. I am rather shy, and this male prerogative of taking the initiative in courtship is a burden, especially in the staid society I inhabit. It is always a ritual and always one must give notice—at least two days ahead for a date, two weeks for kissing, two years for fucking.

But things are a little different now. I am, after all, a "doctor" am I not? Also, the girl I am about to call is foreign—not too foreign, but not from Toronto at any rate. She is British though Toronto has been her home for several years since she came over when she was almost a child. I have learned most of this from Lillian, though some of it from the quiet little blonde herself, last weekend at the interns' lounge.

As I have done in the past, I take a deep breath and steel myself for the embarrassing but necessary ordeal of making small talk and appearing interested in a person when what I mainly seek is ass, although certain criteria must be met. My standards are somewhat different from Tom's whose credo is "if it moves, fuck it," but nonetheless the sentiment is similar.

I dial. Bzzz. "Hello." A small, fine voice answers. It is Ann, herself.

"Hello," I say. "It's me."

"Oh, hello, you decided to call did you."

Hmm, that is kind of an interesting response—like we have a contract.

"Um, sure, I did. How ya doin'?"

"Well, would you like to come over tonight?"

"Oh yes, that's great. No, I mean, how about tomorrow? I'm off tomorrow, how about then?"

"Fine, if you like, see you then."

Instructions how to get there from Mount Sinai. She is way in the east end of the city. No, actually it isn't that far, it just seemed like the east end since I never went to that part of the city in my childhood.

At 5:00 p.m. next day I am off. I hop a streetcar, which travels a circuitous route south and east through an area I somehow have rarely travelled. The weather is warm and pleasant. A nice summer evening.

After a ride, which is shorter than I anticipate, I arrive at the designated stop. I disembark, and there waiting for me at the stop, despite explicit directions so I could have made it to the apartment on my own, is a very pretty blonde girl. She smiles at me and we greet and then head back to her apartment, which she shares with her mother.

As we walk, I savor the qualities of this young woman, age twenty-two. She is very light skinned—white in fact—like Marilyn Monroe's skin but she is finer and more delicate. She is very blonde—I guess a little bleached though she is certainly a blonde anyway, and she has blue eyes and a small nose. She is wearing a yellow skirt and jacket affair, and I cannot help noticing that though the outfit is by no means provocative, the skirt seems to fit very tightly around firm buttocks creating an effect, which was drawing modest admiring attention as we walked along the street. I note also that she is wearing stockings straight and neat, which few natives wore on a summer's day and the effect is modest, attractive, clean, and ladylike, which I like. I am wearing grey pants and blue blazer for my part, which I had worn to the "Movement" the day we first saw each other.

I remark on Ann's stockings and compliment her looks.

"I like your blazer," she replies smiling with a soft voice with its slight British lilt.

At the little apartment, with mother retired after a while to the bedroom, we sip ginger ale with everything in it and Ann puts on a record. It is Beyond the Fringe, forerunner to Monty Python, and is hilarious British humor. I laugh at some of the jokes and pretend to laugh at others. Truly, the humor is superior but my concentration is wavering. I am now savoring a light shot of vodka and orange too and as Ann changes the record to Part II, bending slightly in her bright yellow skirt, I close my eyes and give a silent prayer.

"God, will I ever have that ass?" Her ass is beautiful; I feel a surge of blood concentrating itself naughtily in certain anatomical regions.

I am loathe, however, to make a move. I am still, as ever, paralyzed with shyness. How am I to do this! Isn't it degrading to show someone you like her?

Finally, I resign myself. I cannot break through this barrier. It is now getting late and I might as well give up.

"I guess I'd best go. I'm on duty tomorrow and I have to be up early."

"Oh, I'm sorry, if you must then…."

As I reach for the door with Ann near me I bend down and give her a goodnight kiss. I kiss her rather firmly and… and she returns it forcibly. Well, then I do it again and well, I don't leave quite then.

We are on the couch. She turned out a lamp "for atmosphere" so I turn out the other one for darkness. I have her ass in my hands. I have her breasts. I have her. We are young and eager and ready. But still we do not do it all. We stop. Mother is in the next room. On the weekend Ann will visit me at Mount Sinai.

When I leave I am ecstatic. The electric streetcar winds its circuitous way in the early morning to Mount Sinai Hospital.

IVs and pulmonary edema await, but I have a beautiful girl and we almost fucked on the first god dam date! By God! Wait till Saturday!

9

Saturday

Ann visits me in the residence at Mount Sinai as scheduled. It is just a few days from her twenty-third birthday. We do not waste much time, picking up where we left off at her apartment. This time we divest ourselves of clothing though Ann modestly insists on darkness. We do it. Awkwardly I perform my part, thrilled at my luck. The beautiful body, sensuous and delicate, is clad only in garter belt and stockings beneath me. Clumsily without an instruction book we figure out what to do.

I am quite inexperienced and I am at first afraid she is not, which makes me embarrassed. She seems sure of herself and acts as though she knows what to do. However, as we embrace and explore each other, I find that she, too, has had little experience and though competent, there is an awkwardness too. She catches on fast but she has not done much of this. In fact, I later learn she has done none at all and I have screwed a virgin. She gave up her virginity for me.

As I lie with this pretty girl, a sense of strangeness, of unreality overtakes me. How peculiar to be lying here with the opposite sex. I have never been in this kind of a situation before—and it is exciting and strange. How long I have waited.

But this is a fitting reward.

The sense of unreality lingers—a pleasant unreality. We try it again. Practice helps. I am transported to ecstasy. I do not know if she is too or not.

But after, doubt suffuses me. Were I not a doctor this could not have happened. She is screwing a doctor—she does not care who I am. Like Peter H. A piece of paper how has changed everything. I am the same person. I am angry. But I have worked for this. I have earned it.

For her part, Ann is chiding me. "You didn't even notice me at the Movement. You didn't say a word."

"Silly girl, I was watching you every second."

And Ann realizes that I barely see her as a person. She is a sweet, a candy. She is lovely—a doll, a toy. She is intelligent, I believe (I am later amazed to learn she graduated at the very top of her class from a British girls' school—not a small distinction). It is her body I like, who cares what her brains are. That is not exactly true—I am pleased she is intelligent. It matters more now—but her looks are more important still to a young male chauvinist heretofore deprived, in any case.

There is another quality about Ann, which is a peculiar turn on. There is an unevenness, an unpredictability. I have not known her long, but I sense this. For instance, the way she disposed of Bill. What was she doing at the Movement anyway? She leans left, but she is not really a radical—in fact, she is somewhat politically conservative in a lot of ways. Why is she attracted to me? How is it she is so direct in her interest in me when no other girl I have known has been? She is foreign and exotic in certain ways though a Toronto girl too. She is the opposite of my mother in most respects, yet I seem to confuse her with my sister in my mind at times. I am off balance with her and yet she acts like she possesses me, that we belong to each other. I feel also she could drop me as she did Bill.

My time with Ann is so short. Summer is waning and she tells me in a few weeks she will depart for New York where her sister and brother-in-law now reside and will not be returning to Toronto. I feel an anger at this yet do not tell her not to do it since that would mean a commitment for which I am not prepared. This unpredictability. She is so WASP too; what would my Toronto Jewish family think? I do take her home though, and my mother is pleased. My father, I feel, is less happy. But I learn that miscegenation is at least partly acceptable if the party is either rich or beautiful and Ann is the latter.

I continue to be with Ann constantly over the next few weeks and our lovemaking becomes much more competent and moreover continuous. She matches my passion, and also true to her unpredictability will do things in peculiar places—in public—in restaurants—on streetcars. In the park at dusk she has her hand on my genitals and is performing an obscene act. "Christ there are people around!"

"Don't be a baby—mm." She scares me, but God willing, I give it to her.

Tonsillectomy is in vogue as I am to find when I start surgery in a few weeks and Ann falls prey to this. I visit her in Woman's Hospital and bring flowers. This hampers certain erotic proclivities but seems to enhance others.

Finally, Ann is making ready to leave the city. I do not know if I am to stop her or to go with her or what, but though disappointed and angry too, I let her do this. I let her leave me cruelly alone. How can she do this to me?

"Are you really going?" "Yes, I have to."

The white-skinned pretty girl waves to me. Goodbye, pretty girl. I see her in her yellow skirt tightly stretched across her proud round ass and then she is gone. Will I ever see her again? Will I ever see her like again?

10

The Pacemaker

or, There is No Charge for This

Mount Sinai has a new pacemaker and cardiac monitor and it is my job tonight to stand by on the ward while it is being utilized on a sick patient. The machine is brand new and it occurs to me that the medical department and administration is very anxious to try it out even though the cardiac patient they are using it on is stable and not too sick.

I do, however, assist in setting up the unit and we apply the electrodes to the legs and arms and chest of the patient involved, an affable but worried sixty year old man. Poor fellow, I think we are making him more anxious than ever with all this fussing.

The machine is all set up and it is on. On the oscilloscope a nice cardiac pattern is seen, emitting a constant EKG, monitoring the heart.

Blip, blip, blip, lub dub, lub dub, lub dub, it goes. The machine functions as a cardiac monitor; however, if the heart runs into trouble, the worst being cardiac arrest, a loud alarm sounds and we switch it over to pacemaker, which then delivers a series of regular shocks to the heart making the heart continue beating assisted electrically. Quite a technological gadget.

What will they think up next? Meanwhile I have to babysit this machine on the ward and cannot return to my room tonight.

I am given an empty room next to the patient's room. I am hot and uncomfortable and there are people scurrying around—I do not drop off to sleep for quite a while. Also, with this newfangled machine—what if the poor guy's heart does stop? Geez, what do I do? Have I got it right?

Finally, I drop off to sleep. I am so tired. I am in a deep sleep.

It is a troubled sleep, worsened of course by the situation of monitoring this machine and being in a strange place. Suddenly I wake with a start I am fully clothed and my watch's luminous dial says 4:15 in the a.m. There is a noise like a burglar alarm—a horn sounding and there is scurrying and I see nurses running by.

"Dr. Tozman, Dr. Tozman quickly."

I am half asleep. I am not even sure I am fully dressed. I rush to the patient's room. I look at the oscilloscope in horror as the alarm continues sounding. The green EKG pattern is gone. In its place is a flat green line. Cardiac arrest! The heart has stopped beating. "Pacemaker! On!" I flip the switch delivering a series of currents to the arrested heart to save this poor man, to bring him back to life.

As I am thus engaged, sweating, just awake, I hear "Oooh, ouch ... that hoits ... ooh ow!"

The patient is jumping in his bed. Hey, he does not seem to be dead ... what the. . . . It takes some seconds to dawn on me.

"Oooh, ow that hoits," the vocalizations continue. Dumbly I throw the switch back off and I look at the patient.

"Mr. Green, are you OK?"

"Yeh, yeh, I'm fine now that thing is off." I pull back the sheets and sheepishly I look at the head nurse and she at me.

"His left leg electrode has fallen off, nurse," I try to say with authority. "The machine was not recording his heart because it wasn't connected to it."

Redfaced I calmly retreat hoping Mr. Green won't brain me or sue the hospital. Back in bed my embarrassment suppressed, I manage to fall back to sleep for an hour or two more, which passes uneventfully.

11

Fair Trading

It is late summer. Ann is in New York and has sent me two letters. I reply as best I can but cursorily. I had a romantic correspondence in childhood with Ericka. She is gone forever after all the romantic poems. Besides I am so tired. I am under great strain. My left eye seems to bother me a little at times.

I am on the beach today. I am trying to relax. I am with Gord and two Mount Sinai nursing students, Keira and May. They are pretty girls and my date is a small blonde. She is not as striking as Ann nor as exciting but she is not bad. Gord's dark-haired girl is handsome with a deep tan, and those two seem to be getting on quite well together. I seem to be supplying the girls for a change. Well I guess that is fair play.

As the waves of Lake Ontario crash the shore, I romantically give Keira a kiss and she responds sweetly though without tremendous enthusiasm. As we kiss again, I get the feeling she is tolerating this and virtually in the middle of a kiss I hear a voice say,

"Seymour, will you take me to the September nurses' dance?" She said this out the sides of her mouth with my lips on hers! Shit. What a whore! She is bartering her body for an important dance. How can I refuse? I am angry but I accept. How these women use their wiles. What dupes we men are!

I attend the dance—a nurses' prom. I am introduced like a fiancé and I am thoroughly out of place. I meet the whole nursing faculty who precept all the little students in their pie-shaped hats. I meet other fiancés, policemen, and boys next door.

What am I doing here? At last I can get away. Keira got her escort, but I do not ask her out again.

Ruby, a young, dark-skinned, black-eyed Jamaican X-ray technician, is teasing me in a rather provocative way as I inject IVP dye into an elderly woman. She is making off-stage remarks and makes me laugh and she is quite suggestive.

"Say kid," I say. "Want to come to my room for a few minutes?"

Ruby bats her long eyelashes flirtatiously. "I am off at four," she says. "I will see you then."

I am on duty, but things are quiet for the moment, and after early rounds I repair to my room at the residence. Ruby is already there.

"Hello," she says as I let her in. Larry is just leaving for the evening and winks at me. Ruby is an extremely pretty, black girl. She is slim and supple and well built and she seems quite a little tart. She is a tease too of course.

"Why don't you take your clothes off?" I boldly say. "Oh, you are too fast for me—maybe I will though." "Come on," I coax. "You are such a talker."

"Why I think you are too, Doctor. Would you know what to do if I did what you ask?"

"Try me," I say. I am starting to get annoyed because Ruby at eighteen likes to flirt, but she will not come across. She gives me a kiss on the forehead and I grab her breast and we have a short wrestle. She backs off giggling. I try to ply her with wine and she giggles more, but I see I am merely wasting wine. We are both fully dressed.

Ring, ling, ring. "Hello." Oh Lord, it is Ann. She is calling me long distance.

"What is that noise?" Oh, the TV—I mean radio (I don't have TV).

Ruby is backing out the door—she is really pissing me off.

She slips away.

"Yes, I am working hard (very hard). Are you OK?" Ugh, bad timing. But I miss her too.

Ring, ring. "Dr. Tozman, patient in 207 seems to be going into pulmonary edema. Pulse 140, B.P. 180/110, wheezing—please come up."

I put on my white jacket and in a few minutes am back on the floor.

12

Empathy and Euthanasia

"Empathy, Dr. Tozman, empathy." Dr. Prinz is as usual proceeding at snail's pace through a routine operation and he wants my empathy.

What a little ass he is! I have not slept the entire weekend and now it is 3:00 p.m. Monday and he wants my empathy. I am holding a retractor and staring out the window. How many surgeons take two hours for an appendectomy, I feel like saying?

Last week it was a seven-hour portacaval shunt. Of course the patient died. What a slow poke. He has an FRCS too.

Uncle Abie died. He did not get great benefit from his psychiatric care at the provincial hospital, shock treatment and all. Poor sap. He had a brain tumor. He was admitted to Medicine just as I was going off service. I actually drew blood on him and set up a couple of IVs. Thank God I was off service when he finally died. Hemorrhage into friable brain tumor.

It is fall now. My medical rotation is over, and I have begun surgery. It is grueling, really grueling. Most of it is drudge work—almost all of it is—and moreover we are on every other night, every other weekend.

On duty, one rarely sleeps and on the weekend, though one is first call one day, second the other, if the first call is in the OR, the second call becomes first call. This happens all the time. On Monday we still must put in a full day till 5:00 p.m. or even till 7:00 a.m. depending on the surgery. Thus duty can start at 8:00 a.m. Saturday and continue unabated, with no sleep, until Monday 7:00 p.m., fifty-eight hours.

Utterly exhausting and even inhumane. Many nurses, fresh on duty on an eight-hour shift in our tour of fifty-eight hours, act as though we are as fresh as they and unthinkingly disturb what break we get by phoning for triflings. Some are sympathetic angels and mother us.

In the week, the day begins at 6:30 a.m. when we make rounds on operated patients. At 8:00 a.m. the operations begin and our assignments are posted by the chief surgical resident. At the end of the operative day we do physical examinations on patients to be operated on the next day. As with Medicine, most patients are sick and old. There are less of them dying, by and large; except for the cancer unit and these are mostly terminal operative cases. Most cases die in Medicine, not surgery. Euthanasia is practiced at the discretion of the doctors. Subtle euthanasia since there are laws and ethics. It is a classic form of euthanasia having to do with not treating rather than aggressively treating. We learned this language from a pediatric neurosurgeon in medical school. He often simply would not operate on Spina Bifida infants. These children had spinal tissue ballooning out of their backs through a congenital cleft and were therefore paraplegic. They were not disposed of, they simply did not receive a simple spinal operation, mainly skin closure, and died of secondary infection—spinal meningitis.

An elderly woman has had a laparotomy and was found full of cancer. The operation was open and close and she is terminal and suffering greatly.

"How much fluid is she putting out?" asks the chief surgical resident?

"Two thousand cc."

"OK, give her a liter per twenty-four hours."

Two thousand out, one thousand in. Dead in a day of dehydration.

That is the cancer ward. Smell the stench of cancer. They should have let my grandfather go sooner too.

Most of the patients are sick, so sick. We examine flaccid skin and flabby bodies. How we long for young bodies. A young girl for tonsillectomy. A treat. We draw straws for this.

What a pretty thing. Not sick at all. What different kinds of breasts there are—round and pear shaped, big and small, flat and huge. Nipples are tiny and pink, big and brown. Sometimes half the size of a whole big tit.

A young girl has had a mastectomy. God, not one, but two.

She has had both her breasts lopped off at age twenty-one. Poor thing. Poor child.

"Empathy, Dr. Tozman." In the OR Empathy. Dr. Prinz wants empathy for him after fifty hours of no sleep. What about empathy for me?

13

In the OR

"Cut, Tozman. Cut it. Damn that's too long! Oh no, now it's through the knot! What's with you?"

I am supposed to cut suture ends. "I'm sorry."

There is no sense explaining to Laufer, the chief surgical resident, that I have had corneal transplants and still have quite a lot of astigmatism. Also I am worried because I am getting exhausted and my left eye, which has had a better result than my right, seems fogged up at times. If this keeps up I will be visiting New York for that. Perhaps I will soon be seeing Ann. Also I have applied to Downstate (Brooklyn University Medical Center) for psychiatric residency as well as Stanford and McGill and will be going for an interview before long—if Surgery doesn't finish me, that is.

"All right, Tozman, you can sew her up."

I can sew all right, although the nurses complain I have my face too close to the field. I tie knots and sew well and can now sew my own buttons on my clothes.

Dr. Shapiro is head of Orthopedics. He is a small, bad-tempered, old man and, God, his operations remind me of a butcher shop. He uses hacksaws and real hammers. His rubber mallet broke in the middle of a spinal fusion and he threw the thing clear across the room. Darned if he hasn't got a carpenter's hammer now. I have a particular contempt for Dr. Shapiro because it was he who put my grandfather in a body cast for cancerous metastases, with his diagnosis of disc disease, adding to my Zaida's pain and misery and perhaps delaying anti-cancer treatment. But Shapiro, I learn, does mean well, and he is quite gentle and fatherly on occasions outside the OR. Perhaps he is in the wrong business. He is always available at any time for any reason, unlike dear Dr. Lavin, the excellent orthopedic surgeon who drives a flashy Cadillac and who yelled at me for calling him at 11:00 p.m. when a private patient of his was displaying signs of acute abdomen. "What do you mean calling me at this hour?" I never forgot that and never called him again.

Wilma is assisting Shapiro. She has to stand on a stool because of her height and she is obliged to bend over the field and, oh no I think some perspiration has fallen into the field. Christ, Shapiro has kicked her in the shin! "Why are you so short?" he yells. Poor Wilma. The situation is funny though.

Wilma displays a black and blue mark on her right shin for weeks after.

The most grueling operations of all are the neurosurgical ones and these also seem to be the least precise. They go on endlessly and often I am caught from morning to 7:00 p.m. or later in one of these. The scalp is shaved, burr holes made with a drill, and a square plate of bone pulled out to make a window.

Then operative probes go in. Cutting out a tumor is endless work and I cannot tell what is tumor and what is brain. I sure hope Dr. Schachter knows what he is doing. It all looks like a bloody mess to me. This reminds me of Roy's story at Toronto General. The chief neurosurgical resident was reputed to be a brilliant technician. He performed a fantastic operation, excising a tumor, scooping it out in a few hours where others usually might take six or seven hours to carry this out.

"How did you do that?" Roy allegedly asked.

"When you know what you are doing and are skilled and knowledgeable, these operations are not complicated," the chief neurosurge resident replied.

"You know what the pathological report was on that tumor he scooped out?" Roy reported. "Normal brain. Ha Ha."

Indeed, ha ha, but I sometimes think that's what we are doing here.

14

A Raven Beauty

I marvel at the skill of some of the OR nurses. One of them, Stella, is lovely and her eyes and mine often meet in the course of an operating tour. She has long, dark lashes and dark eyes, which always have a twinkle. Maybe I should ask her to visit me sometime. But things are too hectic to talk in the OR.

Smack—the sound of an instrument slapped onto a rubber glove. "Scalpel." "Suture." "Sponge." Blood sprays into the air—"clamp." One cuts the layers of skin away down to the coverings of the peritoneum, then into that. Retractors hold back the field. All the while we clamp and tie and cut the suture with scissors. Out comes a diseased gallbladder or appendix. The prostates are gory affairs too, and hard work.

I have no chance to make contact with Stella. Lionel flirts with her all the time but he is married. Uh, what a shame.

359, 359. I go up to the surgical floor. The four-to-midnight shift has come on and a new nurse asks me to pass a catheter. It's a post-prostate and there is clotting, which I have to clean out. When I return to the Nurses' Station, I note that this nurse is uncommonly pretty. Her name is Sylvia, Sylvia Germanica, and this is her first nursing job. She is from Winnipeg. She smiles at me and in her starched white uniform, pert hat with its new black band, and proud nurse's medallion on her left breast. She seems an angel. She is dark haired and dark eyed and has full lips. She is slim and nicely built and her skin, by God, her skin is gray. Her skin is the gray of a marble statue. She looks like an Athenian marble statue except that her cheeks have a faint blush so she must be real. I am really taken by her looks and I ask this young beauty to come for a drink with me tomorrow when I am off. She smiles shyly but quickly agrees.

15

A Skilled Surgeon

I am watching Dr. Bohnen in the OR performing an extremely complex operation. I am second assistant and Sam Laufer, the chief resident, is first assistant. I am doing my usual retract-and-snip number, and though I have had little sleep, I am nonetheless fascinated by this particular operation. Dr. Bohnen is the most skilled general surgeon I have seen. His appendectomies take fifteen minutes, more serious problems almost never more than an hour. When I am assigned to him I know the OR time will be short and he is a pleasure to watch. Also, though not warm or friendly, he is nonetheless approachable and never snaps at the interns. He and Sam are chatting as they make the initial cut, incising down to superficial then deep fascia layer by layer. The problem with this particular patient is loss of the deep fascial tissue layer after a series of abdominal operations, and as a result her intestines have all herniated with nothing to retain them. One can see the outline of guts on the flaccid abdominal wall prior to surgery. Dr. Bohnen is going to correct this with a teflon net from the sternum to the pelvis, anchored to landmark points of bone with silk cord. Dr. Bohnen works rapidly and easily. He and Sam discuss the political situation in Toronto and remark on the "rabble rouser" Ross Dawson now running again for mayor. "Those reds want us to work for nothing," Sam is saying.

My ears burn since I know Ross personally, but I dare not put my two cents into this. The "Movement" had turned up a week ago also in the form of Alvin Silver (the retarded mascot) who came in for an ingrown toenail removal. Fortunately he didn't recognize me as

I examined him, or was incapable of that sort of cognition. Later in the OR, as I was walking along the corridor, I came across a patient getting off the stretcher. It was like a ghost getting up, clad in a sheet. That was Alvin. He had changed his mind when he got up to the operating room and wanted to go home. I restrained him.

"Mr. Silver, it's a simple procedure...." "No, no I want to leave."

Dr. Laufer came by just then and, after glancing at the chart to make sure we had a signed consent, bade two aides to wheel poor Silver into the OR where he was zapped with pentothal and the ingrown toenail excised!

In three hours, Dr. Bohnen has completed a very complex surgical procedure and he has left the OR. We give him a small ovation as he departs, and Sam and I are left to sew the patient up. It is a long sewing job, closing the skin, but finally it is done. Dr. Bohnen's operations are so fine—a surgeon makes so much of a difference—a matter of life and death. Other surgeons are often just butchers.

16

A Queasy Boner

Gord has returned from studies at Penn State. Penn State ultimately had a great effect on his life. In his brief time there he met his future wife. But he also organized some left wing rallies which garnered US government attention. Later he was denied a US green card, denied entry and therefore jobs in his narrow field of Metallurgical Engineering.

Arduously then, forced to stay in Canada, he got an MSc. Then with still no good jobs, he even more arduously picked up a PhD at Queens.

At this rate he will be Prime Minister or even President if he can't get a job.

But now he is back and he is very worried. His mother has an abdominal mass and he is afraid it is cancer. Apparently it is the kidney—she has a renal tumor. That is a very serious and ugly business. Luckily Dr. Bohnen is her surgeon—but even he can't do much for cancer.

I try to reassure Gord and indeed take a look at his mother's chart. The findings are grim. She has a provisional diagnosis of cancer of the left kidney and has a huge mass radiologically. I attend the operation, again as second assistant, with Sam there as well. Dr. Bohnen deftly cuts in through the flank with the patient on her side. As peritoneum is opened and the kidney revealed, a massive, smooth round protuberance at the upper pole of the kidney is visible. It does not look too good. But Bohnen cuts into the growth and fluid spurts out.

"It's a cyst, Thank God," he says.

It is not cancer. It is a massive cyst full of watery fluid. I am very relieved and promptly transmit the happy news to Gord who is overjoyed. Days later I am still trying to convince his mother she does not have cancer and finally show her the operative note. Until then she thinks we are all lying to her. However, if she had had cancer we probably would have convinced her otherwise. Or tried.

I am on the ward doing physical examinations. My morning operation was cancelled after we had all scrubbed in. As the patient began to get his pentothal to put him to sleep, he convulsed—a peculiar tremulousness. We were all concerned that he was having a cardiac infarction or stroke or something. He is quiet now and the pentothal is flowing again.

Another convulsion—bizarre, frightening. The IV bottles are checked.

"God, they are mislabelled."

There are two bottles up—one is pentothal the other succinyl choline. They are color-tagged by the nurse, one blue one red— the red for the more dangerous curare-like succinyl choline, which is judiciously administered as a muscle paralyzer to prevent muscular contraction in critical operative situations. In any event, the freely flowing substance was succinyl choline by error, not pentothal. This is technically a nurse's error though the anesthetist is embarrassed by it. The operation is postponed and the patient returned to his room, none the wiser.

On the ward I have done a routine physical and another one is coming up. As I am charting in the nurses' station, I see a young man walking onto the ward carrying a guitar and accompanied by two girls, one of whom is very pretty. I watch the young man with some envy at this retinue since he represents a Bohemian kind of life I never had. He seems personable and nervous and he is my next candidate for examination. His name is Clive and he is a handsome, light-haired youth, very Aryan looking, actually about three years younger than myself. I am amazed to learn he is Jewish.

His harem is deposited in the waiting room as I chat with him in the nurses' station, this forerunner of the Hippies. I see on the chart he is Shapiro's patient, poor kid.

"Look, before you undress why don't I take your blood here," I advise.

He nervously consents and I seat him in a chair in the nurses' station. I take out the needle and syringe wrapped in a sterilized towel and he rolls up his sleeve. Shit, they've given me a 19 needle.

"Nurse, don't you have a 20 needle? I don't need this gauge" "That's all we have, Doctor. Should I send for another?" "Ah, that'll take an hour. OK, I'll use this."

These are our autoclaved needles and the bevels are often dull and this needle's gauge is large. I am getting quite good at bloodletting, however, and I apply a tourniquet, swab and aim.

The needle goes in as Clive sits quietly in his chair. But the damned dull bevel will not penetrate the vein. I see it on the vein (his veins are excellent) and as I push it in, the vein bunches up and the needle won't cut into it. As I am fiddling with the needle in Clive's skin, my classmate Ken walks by.

"How's it going?"

"Hey, listen, Kenny can you get this—I'm having trouble." Kenny starts to fiddle too for a few moments. No luck.

"Here, try this...," I say.

But at this point Clive interjects, "I don't know about you guys, but I'm going to faint"

"Don't be silly, you...."

But Clive faints. He falls off his chair and of course at this point the needle goes into the vein and there is blood all over his arm and on the floor. He is lying on the floor in a dead faint and bloody as his retinue of girlfriends and now his mother and father are peeping out of the waiting room taking in the supine figure on the floor of their loved one being resuscitated by two doctors and two nurses.

"I told him to have breakfast," I hear his mother nervously exclaim.

Embarrassed I help load a groggy Clive onto a stretcher and wheel him to his room where I am able to get a blood sample with him flat on his back. I banter with him further and like his self-effacing Chaplinesque outlook. Poor sap. He fainted when I took blood and he is scheduled for an orthopedic operation with Dr. Shapiro, the bluebeard of Mount Sinai. It is minor surgery, lucky for him; removal of a scapular exostosis—a boney growth on the flatbone of the back—but in Shapiro's hands it will be removed with a carpenter's chisel and hacksaw. I do not tell Clive this and he luckily does survive the surgery. When he is discharged we exchange phone numbers and since we have shared an "emotional experience" together, we become friends.

Perhaps his harem will do me some good. Who knows!

17

Where Were You...?

Late November. I am heading back to the interns' residence to lie down after a hectic OR morning. As I pass by the emergency I hear something going on. Something dramatic has happened and I can hear exclamations and crying. I will be on emergency next and in truth I dread this rotation since again one must make rapid life-and-death decisions.

I do not, however, want to get into something now—I am too tired. I start to move along when I hear the name "Kennedy."

"Kennedy? What has happened?" I ask. "Kennedy has been shot?"

"I am really stunned. You're kidding. Will he be all right? Are you sure?"

"He's shot. He's critical. They say he's dead!"

I am dumbstruck. I cannot believe it. I considered him a Hollywood prince but I had been taken with his charm and wit as we all had. Some of the nurses are crying. I feel weak,

I am returning to the residence. I see Ron Bayes. "Kennedy's been shot," I say. "He's probably dead."

Ron starts to laugh, "Come on, Sy, don't joke. You can't fool a joker!"

"It's no joke. He was shot in the head."

Bayes continues not to believe this, then gradually his mirth is replaced with awe as my story is confirmed by others.

Kennedy is shot and soon it is announced he has died.

18

A Sight for Sore Eyes

I am examining a sixty-year-old man admitted for a cataract operation. Geez, my eyes are bothering me too. I have arranged to go to New York to see Dr. Castroviejo—I have a blurring of my left eye. I can hardly see on it. I am to leave this weekend. Ann is expecting me. Also, I have arranged for an interview at Downstate King's County Brooklyn. The examination of the man is routine. His cataract problem is early so he may be diabetic or have some other metabolic problem. I must be sure to order a blood sugar. I give him a rapid physical, but as I push my hands into his abdomen I note something peculiar. Shit, the guy's got a mass. I percuss his right upper quadrant—a dull sound underneath. He has an enlarged liver! I confirm this, feeling the tip of the liver as he breathes deeply; it is way past his umbilicus. That's trouble. I note this on the chart; put a red mark under my notation and an asterisk. I order liver function tests as well.

Later in the week I check to see what the attending doctor may have discovered. The patient has been discharged. His chart notes only that his cataract was removed. The oculist did not read my note. Great, I am up all night doing this shit and they don't even read my notes! His liver function tests are back and abnormal too though oddly not grossly. Maybe I was wrong then, perhaps I didn't feel liver....

My eye is terrible. I am headed for New York. The last OR days were just awful for me.

"Cut, cut, cut. Tozman, what in fucks's name you doing? Are you blind or what!"

"An intern refusing to take out an appendix? Tozman, I don't believe it!"

Back in New York. I call Ann and take the bus from Idlewilde.

The hysteria of Kennedy's death has quieted. I had seen Oswald shot by Ruby as I watched TV. People were stunned but New York is quiet now.

I am at Ann's sister's apartment in the village and ring the bell. The door opens and even though my left eye is ailing badly my jaw drops at what I see. Before me stands a vision—a veritable feast. It is not the simple, wholesome girl who left Toronto not six months ago, but a shimmering beauty. So stunning is she that she takes my breath away. She is surely something I have conjured, in black clingy dress and white pearls. And her skin is so white it is practically phosphorescent. She looks like porcelain with the fine blue veins visible beneath the translucent skin. I find I cannot speak for a few seconds.

"Marilyn—are you Marilyn Monroe? No, you're better, finer, much better." Damned if she doesn't look like a movie star.

I give a low whistle and she smiles, I play house with this beautiful girl and I expend a great deal of pent up lust and passion. I find Ann's older sister is a beauty also, a darkhaired version of Ann,

Ann delights me, but disturbs me also. She is too much for me.

Am I ready for a movie star? Also, she is far less shy sexually than she was—God no, she's almost brazen. She would only let me see her naked with dim lights, like the TV set on before. Now she walks about nude uninhibited, with feline grace. Her shocking full soft and curly bush fulfilling my fetish, signalling to my great passion.

"How hirstute you are for a little blonde." I am mad for this gorgeous hairiness on a succulent body.

I am revived by my night with Ann but my eye has not improved and I see Dr. Castroviejo's assistant. He is alarmed and therefore so am I.

"Punctate keratitis. How could you let this go so far?" He is angry at me.

"I couldn't get away. I'm on surgery."

"Damn—your eye is more important. You left here with 20/20 vision; now you've got 20/200 in that eye!"

He administers drops and I have to instill antiviral drops every hour for days.

In the midst of this fearsome experience, I take the subway to King's County for my interview.

19

On the Couch

I get on the subway and head for King's County. I am not sure why I am considering this place. Perhaps it is because I do not know much about psychiatry. It barely exists in Toronto in 1963 and though it is my interest and to be my career, I cannot experience it in my internship since an elective in psychiatry is not available at Mount Sinai or possibly anywhere in the city.

All I know of in New York is King's County (Downstate) and Bellevue and I have ruled Bellevue out because of its mystique as a "crazy house" like 999 Queen Street, the provincial hospital in Toronto. I have written to Stanford in California, which has not yet replied and McGill, which has expressed an interest. But I would prefer New York for a number of reasons. Here, firstly, is Ann and then, there is my eye problem and of course there is the intoxicating and bizarre excitement of this melting pot of a city with its massive concrete, steel and glass. I marvel at the bridges and huge skyscrapers, the like of which are nowhere else in the world.

As I arrive at King's County my heart sinks. The hospital facility looks like a huge and run down factory. The ride by subway was also long and unpleasant and I begin to have misgivings that I could never work in this kind of a setting after the quiet, sheltered and clean Canadian environment. Perhaps my interview will dispell this misgiving. The Director, I am told, is absent regrettably and two senior men will interview me instead. One is a fairly young balding man in a gray suit who is smoking a pipe.

The smoke fills the room and I feel slightly nauseous. My eye is blurred and it is stinging some possibly from the smoke. The doctor does not take his pipe from his mouth and after cordial salutations, he begins to question me. He is asking me peculiar questions for a colleague, like—"Why did you become a doctor? Why do you want to become a psychiatrist? Do you like your mother?" Literally. "Do you like girls?"

When I laugh nervously at his line of questioning—I am aghast at this "on the couch" approach—"Why are you laughing? Is this funny?"

I find the meeting humiliating and am relieved when it is over and also angry. The next psychiatrist I meet offers little change of pace. This man is more erudite and likes to show it and when I volunteer that I am creative—I like to paint—he immediately asks what I know about the famous collection, at the Toronto Museum of Art.

"I paint... I am not an art scholar..." I stammer but he does not listen. He goes on to lecture me (poor ignorant oaf) on Toronto's wonderful oriental collection which is clearly his interest and expertise. (I learn much later that he collects oriental art.)

I leave Downstate with a sense of deep discouragement, and fear I will not be coming to New York next July after all. My cousin trained at Mount Sinai, so I go there to speak to the Director. I have heard one must be a U.S. citizen to get into Sinai, but it is worth a try. I see the Director who is likable and who treats me decently, like a colleague, but my information is correct, only citizens can be funded due to a National Institute of Mental Health grant. Dr. Hoffman is gentle with me and indicates he would like to hire me, a Canadian, since he too is Canadian born, now an American citizen.

I feel better after this interview, but am still very discouraged.

I guess it will be McGill. I telephone Ann and break the news to her and she too seems sad. It seems I will be passing up this beautiful girl and my torrid romance.

Disconsolately I am walking along Madison Avenue away from Mount Sinai. I am just wandering to collect my thoughts. I am resigned to the fact that New York will not work out for me and soon I will return home.

I am slowly walking along Fifth Avenue. The weather is nice and I walk for blocks. As I am walking along, I see a small building. It is a flat yellow building with an American flag in front of it. Over the doorway is a red cross. Hmm, a hospital.

A sign on the doorway says "Flower-Fifth Infirmary, affiliated with New York Medical College". In the course of my disturbing interview with the two psychiatrists at Downstate, the more senior man, Dr. Bricken, the art buff, had muttered something very derogatorily about Flower Hospital.

He had said "Now that program is much inferior to ours...." I had barely tuned in to what he had remarked but now the name rings a bell. Flower Hospital is an enemy of King's County!

I walk into the yellow building and ask a receptionist—"Do you have a Psychiatry program?"

"Yes, we do" is the answer. A call is made to Metropolitan Hospital, their affiliate, and I am given an immediate appointment with a Dr. Harold Kaplan, the educational director. I am recruited virtually on the spot and I accept.

"How did you hear of our new program?" asks Dr. Kaplan. "Well, you see, to tell you the truth, I was walking along Fifth Avenue and I saw this yellow building..."

I am cut short. Kaplan wanted me to tell him that Metropolitan Hospital was famous, not that I walked in off the street. I apprise Kaplan of the derogatory remark made by Downstate, which interests him intensely.

"They have an obsolete program, you know," he announces. "They're washed up, have been for years. That's why we are better even than Columbia."

In New York, if you have an enemy, you also have a friend.

20

Fate Has Spoken

I am elated with my luck and so is Ann. We laugh at the peculiar contrasting experience I have had at Downstate and Flower-Fifth. King's County had me on the couch. They treated me like a patient. It seems that is how some psychiatrists deal with their colleagues—we are all patients. Flower-Fifth on the other hand was a hard sell. It was a new program and it was looking for qualified recruits and that meant someone from an American or Canadian school, namely me.

"We like Canadians." Dr. Kaplan had said. Why though, does Dr. Kaplan seem like a vacuum cleaner salesman?

My eye is improving and my vacation is almost over. I have my hands on Ann's silky skin and visually take in her beauty.

"I always wanted to run my hands over the silky thighs of a beautiful girl like you," I say.

"Go and do it then".

And I do it. Ann smiles demurely. I am quite a visual person and Ann looks like a painting. A Renoir perhaps. Her coloring is gorgeous. Her body is like a dancer's, supple and slim with breasts of perfect shape and delicate pink nipples. Her golden triangle is soft and so lush that it shocks one to see it.

There is something so pure about Ann that she is a goddess, an angel and yet there is this trace of perversion, which transports me to incredible thoughts of lust and obscenity for which she is a perfect foil. The Devil-Goddess and I have her.

I must go. I have agreed to return to New York. This means that I will return to Ann. Fortune has decreed it. If I had not taken my idle walk on Fifth Avenue, my life would have taken a completely different turn. By merest chance my return to New York and to Ann -scintillating, incredibly sensuous, strikingly beautiful and totally unpredictable in passion and mood, has become a certainty.

21

Other Crosses

Gryzysyn is showing me where he wants me to stick him. "Here, this is a good vein. Go right in and please don't give me a hematoma."

"Why George, I don't give hematomas. I'm an expert at this." I am still nervous, however, since our blunt autoclaved needles could screw me up.

"Wait Doctor." Nancy the competent Emergency Room nurse calls me. "Look."

"Oh, you Angel. Where did you get this?"

"They came in yesterday. Haven't been distributed yet, but I stole a box."

Disposable needles. Finally, six months into my internship and at last there are sharp disposable needles.

I apply the tourniquet gently to Gryzysyn's upper arm so as not to cause bruising and swab the vein he has advised me to use. In the razor sharp needle goes. I am careful not to exit through the back of the vein.

"Like cutting butter. Wow, what a difference!"

I undo the tourniquet and draw up the dark blood then stabilize the needle in the vein and attach the intravenous tubing to it as Nancy opens the valve and we infuse clotting factor. I banter with George, lying palely on the table, his sallow complexion reminding me of anatomy lab as the amber fluid drips in. Then as the infusion is completed, I deftly withdraw the sharp needle and Nancy slaps a tight bandage on the puncture area.

"There, that wasn't too bad." George says soothingly. He gets up smiling and heads back to his pediatrics ward.

"Poor guy." I say to Nancy. She nods. "I really don't know how he does it."

Gryzysyn is a thin yellow looking intern, a classmate of mine and a hemophiliac. He got through school just like the rest of us and here he is at Sinai doing the same work as anyone. Often I see him limping though and at times he is out sick. A knocked elbow causes a hemorrhage into his elbow joint. How thankful I am my eye condition was curable.

Nancy labels Dr. Gryzysyn's blood to be sent to the lab for monthly clotting studies.

The first two weeks on Emergency have not been as bad as I expected. I keep worrying that a bad trauma case will come in, but those usually go to the bigger hospitals. Dr. Shapiro for all his irascibility has been extremely helpful for broken bones and I can reach him far more easily at his residence than I can get Laufer the chief surgical resident down to help me. Shapiro is always there—a dedicated man—even if he was a butcher in the OR. Orthopedics is a kind of butcher shop anyway. Anybody need soup bones?

Lionel has returned from New York. He went there at my suggestion. "Kaplan is a shmuck." he says. "I don't think I'm going to do it!"

"Come on Lionel." I coax. "It's a good program. It'll be fun. We're a team."

"I think I'll just be a GP." Lionel replies.

But I continue to coax Lionel. I want him to come to Metropolitan Hospital too.

"That shmuck told me I had forty-eight hours to decide. He says someone else—a dame—is flying in from Akron and he'll give the job to her. What a high pressure operator he is," continues Lionel in an angry mood. "Well it's a week now. Let's see if he's still interested."

Later Lionel returns. "Well it looks like I'll be going after all Sy. I guess I squeezed out the dame from Akron." Kaplan had given him the job. "That's great Lionel."

359, 359. I rush to the emergency room. An elderly man. Acute asthmatic attack. He is gasping for breath and is red faced.

"He's not in failure is he?"

"No, doctor. He's been here with this quite a few times. His vitals are OK."

"Alright let's give him some aminophylline and you better give him librium too. Give him 1.0 cc of adrenaline, OK?"

"You mean 0.1 cc Doctor don't you?" "Um, yah, yah, that's what I mean." "Right, 1 cc would kill him." "Right."

Whew, I am glad Nancy knows a few things for she has saved the elderly man and me too.

22

With Tongue in Cheek

I am sitting opposite Sylvia at the Pilot Tavern. I have avoided this place for several months because last time I was here a psychotic individual sat down at my table and began a tirade against doctors and then Jews. By mistake I had let on that I was an intern and that I planned to go into Psychiatry. My ethnicity he quickly surmised since racists have a particular talent for this.

He concluded his tirade with: "We can tolerate the likes of Freud—I mean we can just tolerate him—but you..."

"Sorry Buddy," I say, "I can't help you."

Help him—I'd like to kill him, the sick little turd. I make a quick exit. The tavern is a hangout for the local color, poets, artists, radicals and quite a gaggle of assorted misfits.

Sylvia, shiningly lovely is nonetheless a sheltered young woman. She seems impressed with the action at the tavern and seems also to be rather infatuated with me. She needs reassurance and wonders why I am interested in her.

"What do you mean?" I say. "I like you a lot."

I do not think she realizes that she is exceptionally pretty. Nobody seems to have told her this before. As I look across at this lovely creature with her exotic coloring I wish I could say, "Won't you let me have your luscious body?" But I am afraid she won't let me and I feel there is not much point in continuing to date the pretty girl much longer. She seems to value virginity and wants to marry and have a family. Why don't girls just want to fuck like the boys do? I don't think women really like sex. The ones that seem to just like their power over us men or they do it for pay. Is it because there are less nerve endings down there in the little organ?

Sylvia has a soft sweet body. She is so soft—some women are. I didn't expect her to be so soft—her body looks firm and taut. But I will never consummate my deep carnal desires with her.

359, 359. An alcoholic man has come into the emergency with a severely lacerated cheek. The laceration is through and through as he deftly demonstrates by inserting his tongue right through the hole and wiggling it out of the side of his cheek. He is not in any pain however and our ER staff are practically reeling, ourselves, from the volatile fumes emanating from him each time he exhales.

"Don't anybody light a match." I mutter to Nancy.

Nancy smiles. "Dr. Tozman, I am glad you're here. You are so calm and reliable. A lot of the other interns go to pieces in the ER."

I am taken aback by this compliment. I tend to think of myself as just getting by through the ordeal, and Nancy, the head nurse, has told me she likes my work, and that I am moreover better than some of the other doctors. Is she crazy?

"Nancy, will you marry me?" I say. She is quite willing but explains that her present husband might object.

Meanwhile we are coaxing our inebriated patient to stay on his stretcher while Nancy and an aide try to clean him up. He is bruised, grimy and has clotted blood all over him. Fortunately for him his laceration is not bleeding badly now.

"Don't do that" I say to the man as he pokes his tongue through the hole again. Now he is trying to get up to leave.

"Look, let me sew this up." He is so happy. Alcohol certainly is a good anesthetic.

Now he is being witty.

"You're such a good doctor," Uh, more compliments.

This is really my day. Perhaps Nancy was just flattering me or else she's as drunk as this guy.

"The best I ever had" he is saying as I hold him, one hand on his chest, the other trying to push a suture through his exterior cheek,

"ENT will have to sew up the inside of the cheek. The needle won't hold to the flesh there."

Nancy calls for ENT. An oral surgeon would be better but none is available.

Now the cheek is sewed up—at least the wound is closed. "I'm goin' doc," proclaims the patient. We try to restrain him but have to give up as we are getting backlogged with patients. An FUB has just come in and I have to set up an IV and get GYN. The inebriated patient is up and staggering into the street.

"You're the best, the best I ever had." "Hic."

The FUB is about the fourth I've seen so far in the emergency.

That is a "functional uterine bleeder" and can be very serious if they are hemorrhaging badly. One young woman was in shock and almost died. This one does not seem too bad though very anxious. "How many pads have you used?" asks the nurse. A lot, a lot —I don't know."

GYN is called and the patient moved rapidly to the OR for a dilatation and curettage ("D & C"), my IV dangling from her arm.

I have sent her blood down for cross-match and ordered two liters on standby.

"It's not broken" I tell the elderly little man with the bruised forearm. "It's just bruised." There is no swelling, no linear tenderness and the fall he had was minor.

He is upset at my dismissal of his injury. "You not even gonna X-ray?"

"No it's not necessary. You don't need unnecessary X-ray." "He's not even gonna X-ray" he says to the nurse and to an asthmatic patient on the table.

"You don't need...Oh hell! Send him to X-ray."

And so it goes. In my room, exhausted I drift to sleep and dream exotic dreams of Sylvia and Ann and Nancy and Sylvia and Ann... "The best, you're the best!' Endorsed by an alky derelict.

23

Clive and a Tough Customer

"How does it feel to be on your own...like a rolling stone... like a rolling stone." That is Bob Dylan singing. I have never heard him before nor this song either. Apparently I have been very much out of things. Clive wants me to share this experience with him. He seems to think I will be transformed by this strange singer. I think I like Joan Baez better—her voice is sweeter. I do not seem to be musical and I don't really even care for her that much.

"Where have all the flowers gone?" The radicals like that one—the end of war—yet they subscribe to violence for peace. Human history is so depressing. Will the evolution change anything? And what happens when the terrorists rule—those who kill for a better world, I want a better world too—but must we kill to get it? Perhaps technology will make a better world.

Perhaps our minds will change—we will become smarter and better and more peaceful.

"The answer my friend is blowin' in the wind...."

Why am I not moved? "We shall not be moved." Well I am not.

In the dimly lit room Clive is sitting cross-legged. He is pleased to have attracted me as a friend. It is status to have a doctor friend. He is a highly intelligent boy but a high school dropout. He has a grade nine education and now works for an oil company as a clerk. He hates his job to the consternation of his parents who feel he should make this clean work his niche. His mother thinks Clive is mentally retarded, an idiot, since he has had such difficulty in school and (so he relates) has "failed tests that nobody fails."

"I have failed aptitude tests."

"You don't fail aptitude tests—they test what you are suited for."

"Believe me I've failed them."

Sitting beside Clive are two women, and a third one has just come in. They are all young women and two of them are handsome, one exceptionally so. The two pretty ones talk together cliquishly. The less pretty one talks to me.

I am interested in the dark one I tell Clive.

"Don't bother, she's a very tough customer." His cousin Eddie has tried her out and he knows. Somehow I do not consider this a deterrent and worm her number out of him. Clive's assessment is accurate however I find out later.

Clive has always been considered weak minded by his family. He has been a problem in school and his parents have been informed that he is backward. Remedial efforts have all failed. Yet I see that Clive is in fact unusually bright. Moreover my initial impression of him was that he was a college student, not an idiot and his history amazes me and fascinates me.

"The schools have considered you retarded?" He is an indictment of the educational system.

Clive amuses me. He has a cynical humor and is intelligent and has been oppressed. I like him and he does me. He recognizes my sexual drive and frustrations and agrees to help me out.

"I'd do it for you myself if I were a girl" he puts forth. "Hm some offer. Unfortunately you're not a girl."

He is not homosexual either at least I think not since he certainly likes women. He is very handsome and would have made a very pretty girl. "Yes, too bad you're not—but then if you were you probably wouldn't be offering!"

Clive is being psychoanalysed. He is sold on this and indeed in his peculiar case his psychiatrist seems to be helping him.

He is being advised to enter the new (Toronto) York University as a mature student and his Dr. Jedwab will give him a special letter for the University to consider him. I encourage him also.

"When I was a kid," Clive relates, "I was sent for tap lessons at Jack Lemon Dance Studios. You know," he reminisces, "all the disturbed Jewish kids were sent there for remedial therapy in lieu of a psychiatrist." I smile because my nutty sister took tap lessons at Jack Lemon Dance Studio too. (I remember the dance recital at the T. Eaton auditorium with those children in fluorescent costumes tapping woodenly.)

Clive continues "At one of those recitals, my cousin Eddie (also crazy) and I, were doing a tap duet where you back up, dancing. Well, I tripped and fell on my ass. I was mortified. I was so anxious about the reaction of people that I rushed out into the orchestra and pretended I was a member of the audience. To test the reaction I said to a man next to me— 'Hey, did you see that kid fall on his ass?' and he answered 'Yeh...and it was you!'"

Clive had many rueful and poignant stories of youth—more than I if possible.

24

Doublethink

My days on Emergency are dwindling and Pediatrics is coming up. I can take a breather on Pedes I hope.

I still toy with the idea of a Pediatric career even though I have accepted a psychiatric residency in New York. I was most disposed to Pediatrics in third Meds and got an A in Pedes that year. That was the year I scored on the Pediatric final, the Fibrocystic case-the little blond boy of Irish descent with a hereditary lung disease seen mainly in his ethnic group. He was a pretty child, destined to die within a few years. In my final year, however, Pediatrics was pretty well ruled out. I could not stand to see the poor little kids suffering, nor did I like to do procedures on them.

I also did not care to deal with the worried parents who were much more troublesome than the miniscule patients themselves.

I have had no major trauma cases and no deaths in the Emergency in the five weeks of my rotation. The work has become routine and though I still worry about what might come in, I am more relaxed. It begins to look as though I might make it through my internship.

Byron visited me today. This is a day for clairvoyance it seems. He started asking me about Jerry Cooper a classmate a year ahead of me.

"I haven't seen him for about a year, Byron. Why do you ask?" "I dunno I was just thinking about him."

As Byron is talking, my jaw drops for Jerry has strolled into the Emergency.

"Hi guys, just wanted to see the old ER. Whatcha doin' here Byron?"

"Byron did you see Jerry in the hall?" I ask incredulously. Absolute denial. A strange coincidence. Is it possible Byron picked up a radio signal from Jerry's brain, telling him Jerry was nearby? Perhaps such things are possible. The brain after all is an electrical unit—its electricity can be measured using electroencephalography—perhaps it sends out a weak radio signal. Maybe someday we will be able to communicate in this manner without language.

A young woman has entered the Emergency. She is very neatly dressed except that her hair is disheveled. I am asked to see her. She sits cross legged in black slacks and is smoking incessantly. She eyes me with suspicion, then talks volubly. As she talks the cigarette in a yellow holder waves back and forth from her mouth.

"I have been betrayed," she informs me.

"It is Doublethink. They are out there controlling my mind. You see. It is evident. Do you hear that? They are doing it now."

The strange woman eyes me intently without shifting her gaze. I feel very uncomfortable. I try to tell her to relax and to be more specific and she responds with an angry tirade.

"You doctors are part of the system. Even if you don't know it you are a part of it. Love is hate. It is Doublethink you know."

I beckon to Nancy that we have a looney on our hands.

"She has a psychiatrist on staff here." Nancy whispers and slips me a piece of paper with the name on it.

"What are you doing? Did you think I didn't see that?" The woman is on her feet and angrily snatches the paper from my hand.

"Yes, yes I know him. What are you going to do?" She is suddenly weeping, then stops and begins laughing. Then crumpling the paper she sits staring at the wall, the cigarette in and out of her mouth.

"Excuse me just a moment." I manage to get out of the room and call her psychiatrist. I steer clear of the patient for the next twenty minutes, which is the length of time it takes for her doctor to arrive. She sits staring at the wall or occasionally gets up and walks to the window to look out into the growing dark.

I am very relieved when the psychiatrist arrives. He is a young well dressed man in a natty suit and he sits and talks with her, with myself and Nancy peering in from time to time, ready to do a flying tackle if necessary.

Finally things are under control. She has agreed to be admitted to Toronto Western where there is a psychiatric unit. As the ambulance attendants escort her out of the Emergency, she looks keenly at me,

"Doublethink, doctor. Doublethink. We will meet again. Freedom is slavery. Slavery is freedom." She vanishes into the night.

Is this a preview of my career to be? Maybe I better reconsider this.

25

Gulliver's Travels

I am surrounded by little people. The patients are very small and I do not like to see the little things so sick. The furniture is small and very peculiar, so are the doctors. I am a giant here. I am Gulliver in a Lilliputian world. I never realized before that pediatricians were so small.

Dr. Shapeman is a diminutive person who is also quite nasty to the giant interns. He sits on a chair as he discusses problems in pediatrics, and his feet do not touch the ground. He peers at us in round glasses, and looks to all the world like a Munchkin.

We are however under him, and he holds forth in a thin voice and points and orders. The Pediatrics resident is an East Indian, a woman who is very quiet but empathic to our condition.

Much of our time on Pediatrics is again spent in setting up IVs and taking blood. Here the difficulty is compounded by the tiny veins of the ward population, necessitating going for the jugular vein using tiny intracatheter needles, or if simply bloodletting, from the femoral vein—a tricky business because of the adjacent femoral artery, which would be trouble if stuck instead.

We interns (myself and Lionel) also do physicals as on the other services, and additionally do a number of circumcisions.

Since no aspect of surgery is really my forte, I do not relish doing circumcisions and I regret that there may be quite a few young adults today with lopsided members as a result of my work. My astigmatism makes cutting little genitals difficult for me; however with Lionel and Dr. Bandaree as backup, I manage to muddle through.

"Hey, Laufer was looking for you." Lionel informs me. He looks a little worried.

"Watcha done now?"

"Huh, I dunno. What could he want?"

Laufer is the chief surgical resident and thankfully my contacts with him have been infrequent since I left surgery. I had to call him a couple of times in Emergency. Like the acute abdomen that came in just before I went off service.

That was a forty-five year old man complaining of severe abdominal pain. He was crying out in pain and asked for something for that. His abdomen seemed rigid and he had multiple incisional scars all over it from six or seven previous operations.

"He has adhesions" I told Nancy. "Call Laufer—must be a bowel obstruction."

Though he pleaded for morphine, I held off till Laufer finally came down and that bastard still wouldn't let me give him morphine. The man was screaming in pain and I was getting pretty pissed with Laufer. What a mean bastard. Those surgeons are so hard.

"C'mon Sam he's really in pain. He has a history of bowel obstruction."

"You hold off. Wait for the X-ray." Finally the X-ray comes up.

"There you see. No obstruction." Laufer points out the signs of a clear bowel.

I am amazed since the man has had a history of bowel obstruction.

"Now give him the morphine."

I inject morphine 1/4 IM and before I push the plunger down the patient gives a sigh of relief and the pain stops. "Geez the morphine hasn't even gone in," I whisper to Laufer.

"Yah, he's a malingerer. Throw him out."

The man was indeed a malingerer looking for a fix and ready to be cut open for some morphine.

"Tozman, oh there you are. I was looking for you."

Laufer is looking sour as usual. Geez, what could I have done now?

"You know I thought you guys were pretty much a bunch of fuck-ups. A patient just came in for a portal shunt. He's in complete liver failure. I look in his chart and I see he was just on the surgical unit a month ago and I say to myself: 'Which one of those fuck-up interns had this guy on the unit and let him go by?' And you know Tozman, it was you. Well, I read your note and I must say you surprised me. You picked up that he had a huge liver and you underlined it and put an asterisk. (It was that cataract patient.) So I just wanted to tell you it was a pleasant surprise."

"You picked up the problem and underlined it and the attending ignored your note. That was good work on your part. You saved me some explanations to Lingman."

Sam turns and walks away. He looks as sour as ever. I am mute and red faced. I was braced for a dressing-down and received a compliment. Sam never compliments anyone and he told me "good work."

I cannot believe it. I also cannot handle it.

Lionel comes up to me. "Gee Tozman, are you OK? Was it that bad?"

"Uh, yah Lionel. He said I did good work on a patient on surgery."

Lionel looks at me in disbelief, and starts to say "C'mon stop kidding...," but he stops in midsentence and falls silent.

I resume my work slightly manicky and the day wears on.

26

A Surprise

"Well Dr. Tozman how you doin'?" That is Ruby. She is standing with her hands on her hips and her mouth is open in an insouciant smile.

"Why hello" I answer the sexy little black piece.

I had more or less-considered not bothering with Ruby after her tease number a couple of months ago, but there is something particularly lascivious about her today.

"Say why don't you drop up tonight? I offer. "I just might Doctor," she retorts.

I am now living in the residence in my own room. Larry has moved to another room—I guess we couldn't stand living with one another—and we are paying the extra few hundred for the remainder of the internship in privacy.

There is a knock on the door and there is Ruby. She is wearing a white frilly dress trimmed with lace and it is in stunning contrast to her shining black features. She is truly a lovely ebony creature. A real chocolate treat.

I offer Ruby some wine and she again starts to joke and tease. I feel a measure of irritation rising once again. Damn if she isn't going to pull the same tease number on me again.

I don't make a move. Finally Ruby says, "I suppose you would like me to take my clothes off, would you, Doctor?"

"Sure," I answer. "Why don't you go ahead?"

Suddenly, almost impulsively Ruby gets up and before I can blink her lace dress is off over her head and she is standing in white bra, panties and garter belt. I am boggle-eyed. She then unhooks her bra revealing sweet firm boobs and then slips off her panties, then her garter belt and stockings. She is quite naked. I am clothed and in my whites still holding a glass of wine. Recovering my equilibrium, I grab the naked little tart and kiss her full on the lips holding her firm ass in my hands.

She closes her eyes and lets go. Moments later I am fucking her ass off with great haste lest somehow this dream will vanish.

After this, she fondles my machine, staring at it for some time—she is only eighteen and cannot have seen too many—at least not white ones. Finally she takes it in her mouth and I expend myself there for the first time completing it this way.

"Well you seem to know what to do Doctor" she languidly tells me.

I look at Ruby, nude on the bed lying on her crumpled lace dress. "God you look like a Playboy centerfold." I tell her. Indeed she does, a beautiful young girl, and I have had her quite solidly.

"I bet I surprised you didn't I?" she says shyly.

"I'll bet you did." I answer. It seems she surprised herself too.

27

A Dying Child

It is 4 a.m. I am on the Pediatrics floor attending a twelve year old boy. He is dying. He came onto the service, a strapping athletic youth and though worried, he was in rather good spirits.

Now he is dying. His kidneys are gradually failing and the measures we are taking cannot prevent his inexorable sinking.

It is frightening to watch.

Shapeman is his doctor and Shapeman does not like us interns.

He does not trust us to care for this dying boy. He does not know what we feel. We have not had time to harden and the pain of this boy's suffering is felt by all who attend him. Shapeman has made sure we will be on the floor at 4 a.m. He has ordered IV medication, which only a doctor can give, and the orders read q4h, every four hours and therefore we must be there every four hours round the clock. The Meds could just as easily have been added to his IV bottle but Shapeman wants us to inject it into the tubing instead. He thus has insultingly bound us to the patient who is not even aware of our presence. All that this accomplishes is to make us interns ever aware that we have a young boy who was, not long ago, an athletic bright and vigorous child and who is now slowly fading away. We are forced to view his agony every four hours. On each tour he seems more sallow, thinner and weaker. His skin is bruised and blotched. He is sinking.

28

Hysteria and Placebo

"Well Doctor what do you think is the matter with this woman?" "I think it is mainly hysteria Dr. Benjamin. She says she is paralyzed bilaterally but she can move her limbs if you distract her or trick her into it."

"I think so too. I have known her for years and she has always been a hypochondriac. And now this."

"I'll order her some mild sedation if that's all right and some night meds."

I look at the pale elderly woman lying unhappily in her bed. She seems a little confused and her white hair is tousled. She is not complaining now since she is getting the attention she craves.

Some of the patients here are very confused in their senility.

My grand-aunt was senile when she died. She would have been better off in a place like this I guess. 999 again. The crazy house. Ten days after being admitted there she died. All black and blue. It seems they beat her to death in that place.

For the next five weeks of my internship I am on Geriatrics. In some ways this is pleasant, for Lionel and I are out of Mount Sinai and are based at the affiliated Jewish old folks home in North Toronto. Part of this facility is an infirmary, which we specifically cover and a number of Mount Sinai's attending doctors stop in for an hour or two during the week to make sure things are running well.

One aspect of this rotation involves free meals—rich kosher food three times daily in enormous quantity.

The situation has its attractions but once again it is a worrisome one, for our patients are old and ill and are apt to die. I am hoping I can get through five weeks with no deaths, but the likelihood is not great.

Working in Geriatrics is frightening in certain ways. It is like peering into the future and there is a certain degree of shock to a young person who somehow cannot well conceive of his own death.

The patients are my grandmother's age—indeed her ethnicity—and I see her in them. I see in them also a caricature of my own parents who are not very far off from being elderly and who indeed have acted elderly when quite young. Finally I see in the faces of the elderly my own self—that one day I will be there too.

To add to this horrible reality is the fact that there are two doctors who are patients on the unit and, God help them, they are under my care. Age is a great leveler. One of the doctors, poor soul, is a vegetable; he is Dr. Wallinsak who was a famous Canadian surgeon.

He had written two textbooks of surgery. Now he sits in a wheelchair staring blankly into space. Almost daily his devoted family visits him. They are immensely concerned about his ears for some reason.

"Did you flush out his ears today?" They keep asking me to syringe the wax out of his ears. Somehow the poor souls think his problem is due to ear wax. Unfortunately most of his cognitive brain has gone and he has been staring thus into space for eight years and for all I know many years later, he was still staring into space. And so the mighty fall. And so do we all.

Another doctor is a former gynecologist who is physically disabled but mentally well. The attending doctors are deferential to him and try to include him in our meetings on occasion, but he is ill and not usually up to this. He is really just another elderly and ailing man.

A mustached younger man who has neurological problems from a stroke cries out for medication. He wants his barbiturate. He is given a saline placebo and relaxes somewhat. Placebos are freely given and I comply with the precedent though am slightly reticent. Interns do not have much leeway to question or think. Later I will never give a placebo without informed consent.

Fooling the patient does no one any good. But now we do it.

29

Youth and Power

I'm in the nursing station. Uh oh, here comes one—Mrs. Shapiro. Shuffle, shuffle, shuffle. Mrs. Shapiro slowly approaches the window. "Docta. Docta?"

"Yes Mrs. Shapiro, can I help you?" "Docta I hava pain."

I act sympathetic as one would to a small child. "I am sorry you have a pain—yes, yes."

Shuffle, shuffle, shuffle.

"Mrs. Shapiro, don't keep bothering the doctor."

One of the nurses has belatedly sprung to my defense. I try to indicate that it doesn't matter. The nurse however is unkind and wished to instruct the little old lady. I realize the patients' lives revolve about which shift of nurses is on duty.

Some nurses are exceedingly sympathetic—others cruel. I have experienced this myself, both as doctor and patient. But to be totally under the control of another individual—virtually at a nurse's mercy—is frightening. Some have no sensitivity or concern for the patients under them—the patients are a means for them to exercise power.

We all must have power over something and the elderly serve this purpose—something to have power over. We must be strong. Never, never falter, for our Spartan society loathes the weak even when such weakness is an inevitable part of the course of life.

Today is Wednesday—bloodletting day. Today we take blood on all the patients. Thank goodness I am now adept at this and now we have sharp disposable needles too. This task is accomplished easily and the blood collected in lab tubes for analysis.

"Careful not to break this." Larry had attended my cousin on surgery when he came in for duodenal ulcer and after drawing blood from difficult veins he tripped and broke the three tubes he had collected. The story was still hot with my parents and the family.

As I approach a wizened little man wearing a yarmulke he starts to sob. I am gentle with him and take his blood easily. I finish drawing the blood into the tubes and put a band-aid on the injection site.

"There it's all through Zaida" I say in my broken Yiddish. He continues to sob. I say, "I am finished—don't cry anymore. That didn't hurt, did it?"

"No, No," he says "Ich wein weil die bist so jung." It takes me a second to get what he is saying in Yiddish. "I am crying because you are so young." Suddenly I choke up and cannot speak and I feel like crying too.

30

A Triangle

Clive has come through for me I think. He has fixed me up with redheaded Patricia. I dated one of his girls, the crazy dark one, who cuckolded me promptly with a boyfriend she touted as a cousin. I dropped her like a hot potato. She was pretty though.

"Yah my cousin Eddie tried to fuck her" Clive recounted. "You're lucky she didn't let you. She's ready you know, but she's still a virgin. Eddie says her hymen is an inch thick. When he took her out I asked if he fucked her and he dropped his pants and his cock had a bandage on it. It's true."

Well Patricia doesn't have a hymen. But she's another crazy little bitch. I screw her but I don't much enjoy it and she reports to Clive that "Dr. Tozman can crack his knuckles on his toes." That's indiscreet.

While I am with Patricia, Ann telephones. She is coming into Toronto for the holidays and in fact, is leaving New York and will be in tonight. I talk to Ann with Patricia balefully standing by and then make excuses to get rid of Patricia quickly. She was ready to stay the night too. Actually I am thankful I have an excuse to ditch her.

Lionel introduces me to his father-in-law. He is an impressive man, the Chief Rabbi of Calgary or some such, visiting his daughter and son-in-law. He is originally from New York. I find he is subtly giving me a psychiatric interview but not intrusively and I somehow open up to him.

"Well, you have gone through seven lean years" he interjects. "Now perhaps you will have seven full years."

I am, if anything, anti-religious, but his broad intelligence has an effect on me and he lifts my spirits. Perhaps the next seven years will be full. The last seven were certainly lean.

In the evening Ann arrives and I introduce her to Lionel who is going off duty. He gives me a big wink. The new Ann is a glamorous New York girl, sharply dressed and thoroughly enticing.

She remains with me in the residence through the night and fortunately there are only a few calls.

"Hey, you seem to be putting on weight," she remarks. "I like skinny men, you know."

I am deeply insulted by this. I have been skinny all my life. I thought I would waste away in this internship with the irregular hours and catch as catch can meals. Maybe half coffee half cream is fattening and God, this place with its free kosher food. Ann eats with me in the cafeteria—"Yes, now I see why you're putting on weight."

Her plate is generously piled up thanks to the maternal concerns of the waitresses who eye another person needing to be fattened up. Who was it that said the optimal weight for a Jewish boy is four hundred pounds? Then your mother says "OK, you can stop eating now."

Ann has been and gone. It was so fast I am not sure it happened and I am back at work.

Ruby calls. Now perhaps I can get her up here. But wait, she is in tears. "What is it?"

"Oh, Dr. Sy, I'm sorry I have to tell you..." She is sobbing. "I have been seeing another man and he says he has VD. I like you and I don't want you to have it."

Ugh, so much for that. Now I have to get a blood test. That little slut! All that teasing too. Boy wouldn't that fix me with Ann if I have to tell her to get a blood test!

31

Hysteria and Death

It is three p.m. Visiting hours. I am relaxing in my room for a few minutes when the telephone rings. Of course it is always bad news—the phone is now an accursed enemy.

"Dr. Tozman, right away. I think Mr. Kamen is expiring." I rush to the ward and enter a private room where indeed one of the patients is near death. I jump in and work very hard on the elderly man who is moribund and in pulmonary edema. I cannot find a vein—they are too collapsed and too old. I attempt to do a cut-down on a leg but do not do much better with that. Finally I am able to get a pediatric intracath needle into a forearm and administer appropriate medications by this route leaving a slow IV drip up. After much activity the patient is still alive and seems to be rallying. I am pleased I have accomplished this—saved the man. I have seen a number die this way and this one has survived.

As I exit the room after my ninety minutes or so of feverish work, I see a daughter standing by.

"Is it all over?" she asks, showing fatigue and stress. "Yes," I answer. "He will be all right."

"All right? You mean he is still alive?"

I am momentarily taken aback. Then it sinks in. They want him to die! He is dying and they want it over with. I did not even occur to me not to try and save this man. My reflex action is to jump in and save lives. At first it strikes me that his children are cruel and callous—then I begin to question—perhaps they are right. The man is snoring now—but at best he is barely responsive. What have I accomplished?

To this point there have been no deaths on the Geriatrics service. It is miraculous. A whole month has gone by and there are only two more weeks to go. Will we escape having to contend here with death? As we enter our second to last week, our luck runs out. My patient with hysterical paralysis suddenly expires. Lionel was on duty and attended her. It was unexpected. She has been sent to Mount Sinai for autopsy.

"Somehow, Tozman I'm not so sure your diagnosis of hysteria was right" Lionel tells me. I tend to concede that at this point.

The pathologic report returns. "Cancer of the colon. Metasteses to liver and brain." Her brain is full of little cancer lesions—that is why she was paralyzed.

"What shall we say then Lionel, hysteria with metastases?"

Another bottle of blood for Mr. Zeifer. He is eighty-four years old and is organic. He does not know where he is or who we are. He has a late onset leukemia and we give him one or two liters of blood every other day. There have been articles on blood shortages and requests for donors. I wonder if the donors would be happy with their blood being given in enormous quantities to Mr. Zeifer.

32

The Epidemic

I can't shake this ominous feeling. It is a foreboding.

We have been very lucky on the service of old and frail and ailing people. No one died till the day before yesterday and that is just one. Also I did not have to deal with that, Lionel did, so I am particularly lucky. The one patient who died was my "hysterical" case. But there is something about that death that fills me with dread. I am afraid it is a signal that the flood gates are going to open in the little more than one week we have left. I know this sounds silly, but I have this tangible sensation that a good spell has broken with this one death and that we are in for it. Perhaps I am just getting a little punchy.

It is 9:30 a.m. Sunday. I was off duty at nine but I have hung around talking to Lionel who has had a pretty rough night with his wife. He is shaving and getting ready to go on duty. A call comes through and Lionel is talking on the phone.

"Sy, do me a favor and take this one—I need to shave. It is just a routine. Check it out for me and I'll come up in a few minutes."

Lionel and I have been working well together and in fact, we are going to New York Medical College together come July. I am happy to help him out, knowing he would do the same for me. As he is getting his pants on, I head up to the floor. The nurse greets me.

"Mr. Barney is having some difficulty breathing" she tells me.

I enter his room and he is indeed having trouble. Ugh, he is having lots of trouble.

"Hey, he's croaking." He begins wheezing then stares blankly at the ceiling. Pulse is gone! Heartbeat is gone! "Smack his chest!" Cardiac massage. I press his chest with all my might. A rib snaps.

Up and down I press. But the glazed look remains and he is dead.

"Fuck that Vogel! Help me out—that prick. Now I've got a death and I have to tell relatives and do the death certificate."

"Stand by with librium nurse." The relatives are wailing and carrying on. Lionel has left after giving me his condolences and apologies for the mess, which ought have been his. Oh, well, such are the tales of combat.

My premonition is sadly correct. Epidemic death follows.

They die one after another. While I am pounding Mrs. Sigal's heart, Mr. Zeifer also expires. All that blood for his leukemia and now dead. I declare Mrs. Sigal dead and rush to Mr. Zeifer. I smack his chest too but he croaks.

"Hey, this external cardiac massage isn't working at all." They are too old. I cannot bring them back to life.

Another one. A Woman. I don't know her name. She is gasping. Pulmonary edema. I must get a vein—no veins. A cut down-a cut down. Cut at the vein in her forearm—"Nurse give me a razor." I cut. The blood doesn't even flow.

"Doctor, why don't you let the poor woman die in peace?"

She is holding the woman in her arms. I draw back as though struck and I stand there. She is right—what the fuck am I doing? Again my blind reflex to save is challenged.

Finally mercifully we are off service. I have declared seven people dead, Lionel has done six, including Mr. Kamen whom I had saved for two weeks. All of this took place in the last ten days of a six week stint. Merry Xmas.

33

A Cut Above the Rest

The attending doctors on GYN are by and large a short tempered lot. This is a rough specialty especially as one gets older-only a young man can take it. It really combines two quite separate specialties, GYN and Obstetrics. A physician in this field therefore has to concern himself with the fields of pregnancy and child birth and the different entity of female difficulties. Often an attending gets very little sleep and proceeds to take this fact out on the equally sleepless intern.

As interns, we spend five weeks on GYN and after a two week interlude on anesthesia, I will have another final five weeks on Obstetrics. After that I shall have at last completed my internship and I shall egress from the city whence I have spent my twenty-five years of life. Even now I have my departure papers, which were dispatched by Flower Hospital New York Medical College. I am going to the U.S. as an "Exchange-Visitor" because that eliminates the need for the more complicated immigrant visa and also defines me as a transient foreigner in the U.S., which in the face of the increasing rumblings of the peculiar American war in Vietnam, is the best. At this point I am not even sure where Vietnam is and certain I am not pronouncing it correctly, but I can remember Korea of the fifties and Elvis Presley the soldier and Eddie Fisher and hoards of Orientals. I remember reports that the American soldiers were pushing back the North Koreans and almost simultaneously that China had entered the war. I remember Pork Chop Hill that had been defended (by Gregory Peck?) at all costs only to be abandoned on other orders, later with American dead all over the place. No thank you—I must steer clear of that craziness.

My visa status means however, I must leave the U.S. for two years after I train there, so I will probably return to Canada at some point, though where or when I do not know.

Considering my youth and my insatiable hormones, one might be surprised to learn that I find GYN a not especially pleasant service. I gain from my experience here and I find that it is an advantage to know about women when one wishes to make out with a member of the species. However facing the mysteries of women so explicitly, or I should say having one's face in it, is more of a turn off than a turn on. The clinical situation to me at least, is rarely if ever erotic and I have no desire for so close a look at the object of my lust. Moreover, many patients are quite sick and the tumors, condylomata, fungal disorders and yes cancer too are thoroughly anti-erotic and too frequently horrifying. The "crotch-rot" we witness is a great shriveller of men. I suppose there are erotic possibilities, at least in fantasy, of women submitting so to men. "Either you become horny all the time, or swear off the stuff altogether."

GYN is essentially a surgical specialty and though not as taxing to us interns as General Surgery, we are nonetheless back in the OR and spend much of our time assisting in hysterectomies, ovariectomies, tubal ligations, prolapses and the like. There are also many—too many—exploratory operations for vague female complaints and there is often nothing wrong.

I am assisting in an operation. The figure on the table naked anesthetized and shaved, is a pretty young girl. I note her angular lovely body and firm pubic mound. I am in third position at the operation; the Gynecologist Dr. Morrow and a surgeon Dr. Baker are performing the operation.

Dr. Morrow had seen the woman (girl in fact—seventeen years old) one week before. He had done a dilation in his office for reasons, which are unclear to me; subsequently she has complained of severe abdominal pain. It is true she could possibly have a ruptured ovarian cyst or appendicitis, but it occurs to me she could also simply have a stomach ache from manipulation of her interior a week earlier. I assume these doctors know what they are doing. I guess her abdomen is board rigid and she has a high temp?—or something, hasn't she?

Dr. Morrow and Dr. Baker are joking with each other. They decide since the patient is so young they will do a "bikini incision". That is they will cut her horizontally, below the pubic line, so the scar will not be evident. A difficulty with this incision is poor exposure of the higher structures—the gallbladder, appendix, kidneys—though the reproductive organs and bladder can be visualized well. Dr. Morrow cuts, then, transversely below the hairline, above the smooth pubic mound. Cut, clamp. Tie the vessels. Down to superficial fascia. Cut fascia. Down to peritoneum. Clamp and tie off blood vessels. The reproductive organs are now exposed—I am retracting back the incision. Dr. Morrow feels the uterus and ovaries—normal. He has a look of consternation—Now what? There is a moment of indecisiveness. Dr. Baker suddenly takes command.

"We have no choice—we have to look higher up." Now Dr. Baker takes over. He momentarily looks at the neat transverse incision and then at a point intersecting two third to the right he brings the scalpel down and makes a sweeping vertical cut, from the transverse incision, circling up around the umbilicus and ending at the sternum. The poor lovely girl is now cut in an inverted T from the pubic region to the sternum. I feel faint. She is going to have a horrible scar.

Dr. Baker examines the appendix, gallbladder, kidneys. Normal. Everything is normal. Her normal appendix is removed.

Then she is closed up.

A pretty seventeen year old girl has a huge T shaped incision top to bottom, defacing her for her life. There was nothing wrong with her! She had had a stomach ache and now has a huge cut. I can hardly speak. I feel ill. Dr. Baker and Morrow seem dejected too. Why did they have to operate so quickly?

Another operation. Dr. Landsky. He is a tall man who does not seem like any great genius to me. An exploratory lap once again. Presumed ovarian tumor. A thirty-three year old woman is cut open.

There are no abnormal findings. "I guess I should have cleaned her out better" he remarks. He apparently mistook fecal matter in the gut for an ovarian tumor. Sew her up.

34

Ward Work

After making evening rounds, I examine at the nurse's request, a young woman who has just had a D&C. She is complaining of abdominal pain and I feel her abdomen. I see little wrong with her, kid her for a few moments and leave prescribing a sedative.

I make an entry in her chart and as I do so I note on the face sheet that she lives nearby and that her number is easy to remember PA5-2555. Her name is Toni Smith.

A few days later, knowing the patient has been discharged in good condition I do something I had never done. I call up a patient I saw on the wards and I ask her if she would like to go out with me.

"Do you call up all your patients, Doctor?" she asks.

"Well, you weren't my patient; I just gave you something for a tummy ache". She seems pleased that I have called her and I see her for coffee. She is a very attractive brunette with long dark lashes and brown eyes. I do not attempt to do anything with her on this first date but make a move on the second, at my place.

Suddenly Toni becomes livid. "Oh, you're just like all the rest! All you want is a piece of ass!"

I am nonplussed. I thought she was willing—even provocative.

Now she is telling me I am like all the rest. "Damn it—of course I'm like all the rest!"

That is a sort of compliment to me for I have been so sheltered and sexually backward till this very year that I do not mind being "like all the rest". But Toni refuses to come across. She is angry. She talks of independence, being a sex object and of marriage. She is interested in marriage. I just met her and she wants to marry me. Fuck her. A real Toronto girl. I do not call her again.

Another call to the floor to see a patient. This one is a two a.m. call. Wearily I go up to the ward. It is not a great emergency, but some IVs need reinserting and I can write some orders. I do the work and sit down for a few moments in the nurses' station. There are two nurses on duty and I banter with them for a little while in the early morning hours. One girl is new and she is covering GYN tonight. Actually she works in the Pediatric Nursery. She tells me she is not on GYN normally. She is an attractive sweet blonde girl and she tells me her name is Anne. Anne Petersen.

"Where are you from?" I ask for she has a soft accent.

"I am German" she replies almost embarrassedly. I am attracted to this sweet woman even if she is German and next morning I call central nursing, identify myself and ask for Anne Petersen's telephone number. Since I am a doctor, the number is readily given to me and I call Anne up.

Perhaps fate has decried that my best women must be Anns or Annes?

Anne is very surprised I have called her. She seems incredulous in fact. God, I had even actually met her. When I telephoned Sabrina the Sabra I had never even seen her—I was just going on Larry's recommendation. I am basically so shy, but this drive, this inexorable drive—the quest for ass overcomes everything. I am governed by impulses, which control me on which I must act, or die.

35

Anne

As my internship is proceeding to a close and the world outside awaits, Anne comforts me. She is decent and gentle and maternal.

My affection for her increases and we are together constantly.

She is highly intelligent and therefore not happy as a nurse though there are brief moments of satisfaction in the profession, she relates.

Anne tells me she is German and Byron who bears the torch for the holocaust chastises me for seeing a person of such national origin. He does not see that the fineness of some of the young Germans, young who so regret what their people, their fathers, have done that their lives are spent in apology and hopes of making up for such horror. They are innocents. The guilty have no regrets but the innocents have guilt. Moreover, I find to my surprise that Anne's father is in any case Danish, not German and was in fact a part of the Danish resistance.

His wife was German and they later settled in Germany where Anne was born. During the war they were in Denmark. Anne however considered herself German and accepted the responsibility and guilt for what the Germans had done though totally decent and innocent and even on the opposite side, one could say. Such is the perverse way of the world.

Now, how odd! I learn that Anne has had a corneal graft just like me! God that is unbelievable! What a thing to have in common.

We discuss our operations. She has had a round graft, mine are square. She also has keratoconus though only in one eye and has had a perfect operative result too. A million to one coincidence.

My affection for her increases. But is that not also another perversity of fate? For did not Dr. Taubee in LA warn me about eyes?

"Marry someone with good eyes" he had advised somewhat ominously at the time. "Don't marry a nearsighted girl." And here was Anne, with my very condition....

I find with Anne, some two months before I will say good-bye to Toronto, a strange peace and contentment, which I have rarely experienced before in my life. I have an emotional bond with her— surely a type of love. But soon I will be gone—and there is Ann—what of her? These are two such different women—my women—must I choose between them? Must I make a choice?

Anne calms me. She is so tender. She mothers me and is a gentle sister. She understands me, cares, and I understand her. Ann unnerves me. She is dazzling, beautiful, unpredictable and turbulent. She unsettles me—and yet I am drawn to her and she excites me.

I am so bad at this—a real bungler. My experience is so limited. What am I to do?

I loved sweet tender Anne. On my last night together as I lay with her and she caressed me, not knowing what the future would bring, I suddenly found myself in tears. And as she gently stroked me, and we kissed, she whispered, "Please don't ever change." The poignant anguish of that moment was never lost.

She so easily let me go. Perhaps she should have fought harder. She was too gentle. She could have won. [You can love more than one and differently. I wish I could have had them all].

I am soon to go off service. I attend Saturday morning GYN clinic, which we are not obligated to attend and I find none of my cohorts are present.

"Well," the attending gynecologist remarks, "You will learn and they won't."

I smile and reply—"Do I need this? I'm going into Psychiatry."

He laughs.

I examine a patient for the GYN man and return to give him my findings. I have assessed the case pretty well I feel and begin to tell him about it.

"How old is she?" he asks.

"Um, I'm not sure—maybe fifty...."

"You didn't ask how old she is?"

Suddenly this doctor is dressing me down. He is using my words against me. "I don't care if you are going into psychiatry! You conduct a proper examination!"

I have showed up solo to an optional weekend clinic and this is my reward! The chastisement has no correspondence to reality-it is simply a nasty outburst from an overwrought attending doctor. But I do not return to any more optional clinics and never pass another word to this man in the next and final eight weeks of internship.

36

More Slight Mistakes

Anesthesia is a two week interlude. It is almost a vacation since I am not permitted to take much responsibility. Largely I observe operations and fiddle with the anesthesia machine under explicit instruction. Night duty is, for once, easy and I am rarely called for emergency operations since the anesthetists do not really need the interns. Therefore I am able to sleep and to see Anne. I have lately had less letters from Ann. She called a week or so ago, but seems more distant—I have a feeling she is up to tricks in New York. But I will be there soon.

I am at the topmost end of a GYN patient, with the anesthetist. Dr. Landsky is operating. I have assisted him in the past when he made the exploratory laparotomy on the young woman for "ovarian tumor". "Oh, I guess I didn't get her cleaned out enough" he had said, having felt fecal matter and, concluding it was a tumor, then operated.

Now he is operating again. He doesn't recognize me since I am gowned and working with the anesthetist. He opens the woman's abdomen and damned if he does not say: "Oh, no tumor—I guess I didn't have her cleaned out well enough." He has done it again, cutting up a young woman for no reason because he is too sloppy to "clean them out" and he mistakes fecal matter for tumor. I am shaking with anger but can do nothing. God, I have seen him operate—how many times? Five? And two of these were totally unnecessary. How many young women has he cut up, this Jack the Ripper?

37

Birth and Rebirth

There is something about this final service of my internship year that fills me, (though comingled with anxiety and dread that I will not be adequate to the job at hand), with an exuberance I have not felt on any other service or even before in medical school. Suddenly, at the end of my medical apprenticeship, I am no longer dealing with death, but rather with the origins of life—with life itself. Promptly I am immersed in hard-exhausting work once again, but I do it willingly with a different spirit.

This is my last five weeks as an intern and of course this contributes to the euphoria. Also I seem to be regarded now as knowledgeable and expert. "Those interns can get veins anywhere", a friendly obstetrician Dr. Tancer remarks appreciatively as I slip a needle in smooth as butter. Suddenly what was difficult to the point of desperation at times has become almost astonishingly easy.

Also in the delivery room, the midwives imported from Britain who themselves can deliver babies better than a lot of the doctors, treat me well. "The nurses in delivery won't call you if they think you are no good. Or they will call you too late and you arrive after the baby is delivered by them." They are calling me on time however and I am involved in numerous deliveries with the residents and attendings as backup.

I love the OB service—if that is a proper word. Certainly the contrast to the confrontations with death is a remarkable thing. There is still certainly drama.

A forty seven year old woman is in shock. She has been crossmatched. "She is losing too much blood." She is Catholic and this is her eleventh child. Finally her tubes will be tied at medical insistence, for another child will kill her. Blood is given and she rallies. The child is normal.

There are no deaths on the service. There is little misery.

Perhaps I am just lucky with this.

I watch the head of a child crowning. Just as it does, I make an oblique episiotomy incision. The specialists do a vertical incision, which is neater "cosmetically" and heals better, but there is a danger of a rectal tear and I do not need that. The head crowns and turns. It is being expelled in classical fashion. One shoulder emerges then the other, then the torso comes up and out, umbilicus dangling. We clamp the umbilicus twice and cut between and the baby is free. Nurse has got him—it's a boy. Mother is exhausted but smiles. She has had a epidural and is awake. Toronto is a forerunner of epidurals and we are proud of this method.

The placenta is next extruded with some blood and after cleaning up the patient, I sew up the episiotomy, neatly and quickly. I am good at sewing having done so many incisional closures on surgery—and the procedure is complete. We take the patient off the stirrups and she is wheeled to recovery.

At times I drop by the nursery for its pleasant atmosphere and I see Anne maternally feeding one of the little creatures possibly that I helped bring into the world.

I like obstetrics best. But I will not be an obstetrician.

Gynecology is part of the package and I have no liking for that- an aspect of surgery. Also I see that the obstetricians with some exceptions like Dr. Tancer are very paternal to their patients and very nasty to the interns and even to the residents. Dr. Lebow criticized the Pakistani OB resident yesterday and there was almost a fist fight—hysterical denials. I guess it was a loss of face or something for Dr. Buri to be criticized. Dr. Lebow was taken aback and sullenly muted his professional (and I guess patronizing) suggestions.

I observe one stillbirth in these last five weeks. Thankfully it is the only one I see. The infant is dead and has been apparently for weeks. It emerges at labour time like toothpaste from a tube, a horrible flat pasty substance, not human.

Several deliveries are breech and this requires more experienced doctors than I. These are tricky deliveries. Some babies are "transverse lies" and will not deliver normally. Some are too big for the pelvis. Sometimes a flaccid uterus will not contract enough to extrude the child—that is called dystocia.

All these must be delivered by section.

The weeks pass. A pretty woman in the labor room flirts with me. I am amused that she is doing this, for her belly is round and full with child and she is flat on her back. She tells me to visit her when she delivers. I do so and she presses her phone number into my hand. Apparently the father has vanished and she is looking for action. My time now is short and after one try at someone's patient, I have no intention of doing that again. Mind you she is pretty—and wild too. Unfortunately too crazy, I decide.

Sylvia calls me. Lovely Sylvia with her marble features and grey skin. Grey is not my favorite color for flesh but her coloring, with the healthy rosiness too, is exotic. She is so pretty. "Why haven't you called me? Have I done something wrong?"

I realize Sylvia has an infatuation with me. She is serious.

I kiss her—she is so soft.

She is offering herself to me. "I am yours" she is saying.

And I decline. Again I decline when something like that is offered.

And suddenly—quite suddenly—a frail craft that has ridden the harsh rapids is quite, quite, becalmed.... It is all over.

PART IV

EPILOGUE
Amerika, Amerika

We have passed through Buffalo and are heading for New York.

I am travelling with David Naiberg a classmate of the year ahead who was a first year resident on surgery. He is driving to New York and I am accompanying him. I have a knapsack and a suitcase. My exchange visa has passed immigration and in eight or nine hours we will be in New York.

David is going into ENT. He will be at Manhattan Eye and Ear, having completed his required one year of general surgery. He is married and his wife is just about due to deliver so she is staying behind in Toronto till David sets up in New York. We joke about celibacy during pregnancy and how his wife will be getting it in spades soon.

I am heading for New York. Lionel is coming separately to the Metropolitan Hospital affiliate of Flower-Fifth Hospital. We have learned also that the girl from Akron who was trying for Lionel's position who he allegedly had "cut out" by accepting Flower's residency, was also coming to Flower-Fifth. Lionel and she were both accepted—they were not competing for positions—that was Kaplan's con job.

I have left behind Anne—tender gentle decent Anne. Yesterday I said good-bye and I cried and she cried. "Don't change" she whispered. "Please don't change."

"I will never hurt you" I vowed. "I won't change."

How could Anne have asked me not to change. I care for her. She is one of the last people in the world I wish to hurt. But I am hurting her. For the very people we wish least to injure because of our deepest emotions, are the ones we can hurt the most of course.

So I have caused pain—am causing pain.

Ann is in New York. She represents something else. Perhaps she is a Lorelei. She is glistening, beautiful, chimerical.

Perhaps she is leading me astray. Her attitude towards me seems cooler of late. What is she up to? Does she think I am another Bill? I think she is up to tricks in New York. I shall have to take care of that.

The car speeds along the American highway amidst the crowds of other vehicles. I am travelling farther and farther from my home, my family, my roots. I am in a strange country going to a strange city. It is frightening and bizarre. I am intoxicated by the American turbulence. I am no longer in the country, which is in the shadow of the American giant. I am inside the giant itself. There are frightening sounds of war—there are noises.

There is danger—socially, professionally. Here, there is the very best that civilization has to offer. And the very worst.

Before long I see the massive skyline of the turbulent intoxicating city beckoning me—calling me to what? The Lorelei calls and the poor sailor follows. The city will swallow me into its grinding bowels. I am a new doctor. I am very young. I have barely lived. I have barely seen the world. I am from a staid and calm country, from a quiet city. Am I matter travelling into antimatter? I am a child. I am a child no longer.

The End.

In Memorium

To Gord Rosenblatt and Lawrence (Shendy) Shendalman
My eminent and beautiful friends - more than brothers.
I loved you guys.

Toz

www.ingramcontent.com/pod-product-compliance
Lightning Source LLC
Chambersburg PA
CBHW050632160426
43194CB00010B/1633